THE PURITY CODE

Books by
Jim Burns
FROM BETHANY HOUSE PUBLISHERS

Accept Nothing Less
(available Fall 2008)

*Confident Parenting**

*Creating an Intimate Marriage**

The Purity Code

Teaching Your Children Healthy Sexuality†

*Audio CD; DVD & Curriculum Kit also available
†Parents' Kit also available: *The Purity Code,*
Teaching Your Children Healthy Sexuality,
and special Audio Resource CD

JIM BURNS

THE PURITY CODE
GOD'S PLAN FOR SEX AND YOUR BODY

BETHANYHOUSE
MINNEAPOLIS, MINNESOTA

Published by Bethany House Publishers
11400 Hampshire Avenue South
Bloomington, Minnesota 55438

Bethany House Publishers is a
division of Baker Publishing Group, Grand Rapids, Michigan

Printed in the United States of America

In keeping with biblical principles of creation stewardship, Baker Publishing Group advocates the responsible use of our natural resources. As a member of the Green Press Initiative, our company uses recycled paper when possible. The text paper of this book is comprised of 30% post-consumer waste.

g green
press
INITIATIVE

Library of Congress Cataloging-in-Publication Data

Burns, Jim, 1953-
    The Purity Code : God's plan for sex and your body / Jim Burns.
        p   cm. — (Pure foundations)
    Summary: "Family and parenting authority Jim Burns explores the tough and sensitive issues of sexuality, preparing preteens for their adolescent years. Presents biblical values about sex, bodies, and relationships"—Provided by publisher.
    ISBN 978-0-7642-0209-4 (pbk. : alk. paper)   1. Sex—Religious aspects—Christianity—Juvenile literature.   2. Sex instruction for children.   I. Title.

BT708.B8825 2008
241'.66—dc22

2008003433

To Steve and Sue Perry

*I treasure our years of friendship. You inspire me with your
dedication, generosity, passion, and fun-loving spirits.*

Acknowledgments

Thank you . . .

Cathy . . . *After all these years, we still are trying to help kids make good decisions. Thank you for the decision you made to be my bride and be a wonderful example of living the Purity Code.*

Christy, Rebecca, Heidi, and now Dave . . . *I am the most fortunate man in the world to live my life with you. No one said it would ever be boring.*

Dean Bruns . . . *Your partnership in ministry and ever-growing friendship is one of the highlights of my life.*

Rod Emery, Rick Haugen, Randy Bramel, Lucie Moore, Geoff Moore, Bill Bauer, Bob Howard, and Jeff Armour . . . *There has never been a more effective Executive Committee in the world. Your support, belief, challenge, and commitment truly amaze me.*

Kyle Duncan, Greg Johnson, Natasha Sperling, Jeff Braun, *and anyone else who worked on* The Purity Code . . . *You brought this dream to life. May thousands of kids make the Code a part of their life. Thank you also for your patience with a "flakey writer."*

Cindy Ward . . . *Once again we finish a project together. You are a precious gift from God.*

Contents

A Note to Parents

The most effective sex education takes place when parents talk with—not to—their children about sexuality-related issues in an authentic manner. This is never easy and sometimes embarrassing, but parental involvement makes all the difference.

I wrote this book from the standpoint of a dad talking with his son or daughter. I have tried to address all the issues of today. Some parents may think the information is too blunt while others may think it is not direct enough. Your job is to adapt the material to fit what you believe is best for your kids. Nothing will replace the conversations you should have with your own children.

The most effective way to use this book is for both the parent and the child to read one chapter at a time, going through the questions at the end of each chapter before moving on. Some parents will literally read the chapters out loud with their child; others will read chapters separately from their child and then talk. Frankly, the dialogue that will follow is more important than what I have written, but the information here provides a foundation for those conversations. Even the manner in which you dialogue is important. Kids learn best when they talk and you listen. Don't use this as a chance to lecture. (That was my job!) Your job is to create a safe, loving environment to open up the conversation with your child about the life-changing subject of his or her sexuality.

Some churches and groups will use this book as a curriculum. I'm excited about that. And yet, it is my hope that at least part of the teaching will include parental involvement.

The Purity Code Audio

A supplement to this book may be very helpful to you. We have produced two incredible one-hour CDs on the Purity Code. The student version is meant to be listened to by parents and their children together, and it was created to encourage dialogue. I invited noted experts in the field of sexuality to join me in pertinent discussions about various topics from the book. Some of the conversations were adapted from my daily radio broadcast heard around the country. Overall, the recordings are compelling and a bit entertaining, and again, they are provided to give you more opportunity for dialogue. The other CD is for parents only. I think you will find both CDs very much worth your time.

THE PURITY CODE

CHAPTER ONE

Introducing the Purity Code

Purity: Freedom from guilt or wrongdoing; innocence; virginity; physical chastity; freedom from inappropriate elements; virtue; the state of lacking a moral wrongdoing; honor.

Code: A set of standards to live by; a system or collection of values and regulations.

A growing movement of people your age are committing themselves to something called the Purity Code. They're going against what society considers "normal," and they're making a radical commitment to God, their family, and their future spouse to live a life of sexual integrity and purity. It is one of the wisest decisions they will ever make, with far-reaching positive results.

Did you know that the decisions you make today can affect you for the rest of your life? And deciding to commit to the Purity Code can even affect your future children and your children's children. I know that sounds almost too serious to handle, but following the Code really does make a difference.

The Purity Code is not just about sex. It is about living in a way that can bring you the most freedom and set your future up for joy. People who live by the Purity Code carry the least amount of spiritual and emotional baggage (bad memories, regrets, etc.) into relationships and their eventual marriage.

Thousands of people before you have committed to the Purity Code, and although some later compromised their commitment, I have still never met a person who regretted making the initial commitment. In fact, they say it is one of the best decisions of their life. A commitment to the Code is not always easy; the temptations to break the Code are everywhere. But with God's help and your wise decisions, you can live life as it was meant to be lived.

Here is the Purity Code:

In honor of God, my family, and my future spouse, I commit my life to sexual purity. This involves:

- Honoring God with your **body**
- Renewing your **mind** for the good
- Turning your **eyes** from worthless things
- Guarding your **heart** above all else

Well, that's it. That's the Purity Code. Looks and sounds pretty easy, doesn't it? Actually, it takes an incredible amount of faith in God and a lot of self-discipline to make the Purity Code a way of life. But then again, good things almost always require effort. People who do best don't follow the Code just to please their parents or because everybody else is making a commitment. They take the time to seriously consider this very personal decision. Then and only then, when they truly understand what is involved, do they commit to the Code.

If you decide to live by the Purity Code, you will need to give four areas of your life to God for His help and strength: your body, mind, eyes, and heart.

The Purity Code is very closely linked to your relationship with God. The problem is, at the same time that your body is changing and you are rapidly moving from childhood to adulthood, your relationship with God is probably changing. At one time it seemed so simple, didn't it? And yet for many people your age, faith now seems a bit more complicated. As you examine the Purity Code and your relationship with God, don't think you have to have it all figured out. God is eternal and all-knowing, and you, well, aren't. (And neither am I!) If it is a bit foggy right now, believe me, it will become clearer as time goes on. Thankfully, the Bible, written so many years ago, is filled with the answer to the Code.

Jesus was once asked a very important question: *"What is the most important commandment?"* Without hesitation He said, *"Love the Lord your God with all your heart and with all your soul and with all your mind and with all your strength."* The second most important commandment, He said, is *"love your neighbor as yourself"* (Mark 12:30-31). Some people call this the "Jesus Creed" and believe it contains the most significant words Jesus ever said. These simple directions are definitely essential to understand and live by. They also summarize the Purity Code.

Honoring and loving God with your body (strength), mind, eyes (soul), and heart is really about living a life of purity. We do this in more ways than just our sexuality, but everyone would agree that a pure life includes sexual purity. Even the statement about loving your neighbor as yourself fits perfectly with the Purity Code. By living a life of purity, you are not only caring for your relationship with God, your family, and your future spouse, you are caring for others who will look to you as a role model and not causing them to stumble in their future relationships.

Each year when I was a youth worker, I would talk with students in my youth group about the Purity Code. Scott and Anne didn't know each other back then—they weren't in youth group at the same time—but they separately made commitments to live according to the Purity Code. After college they met and fell in love. When they decided to get married, they asked me to officiate at the wedding. What a privilege!

Before the big day arrived, we spent time together in premarital counseling, and I asked them about their sexual purity. They both talked about making a commitment to sexual purity at a young age and then keeping it. They had honored God, their families, and each other (before they had even met) by committing themselves to sexual purity.

Their wedding day was one of the most joyous days I have ever experienced as two incredible people pledged their love to each other. Today their marriage is strong and secure. Sure they had temptations before marriage, and still do, but with God's help and some strong doses of discipline, they are living a life of freedom and enjoyment because they honored God with their bodies, they renewed their minds for the good, they turned their eyes from worthless things, and above all else, they guarded their hearts. You can do the same!

Honoring God With Your Body

"The body is not meant for sexual immorality, but for the Lord, and the Lord for the body" (1 Corinthians 6:13). If you decide to make the

Purity Code a part of your life, you will need to commit to honoring God with your body. One of the most incredible concepts stated in the Bible is that *"your body is a temple of the Holy Spirit who is in you, whom you have received from God"* (1 Corinthians 6:19). This means that for those who believe in God, He actually resides in your body— in a very mystical way. So it is only natural that we would want to honor God with our bodies—to literally commit our bodies and lives to Him. That means keeping ourselves as healthy as possible by eating well, exercising, getting enough sleep, and staying sexually pure. Even cleanliness is a sign that we are taking care of this gift from God.

On the other hand, those who don't follow the Code will possibly give their bodies sexually outside of marriage. They may fill their bodies with unwholesome ingredients, including alcohol and drugs. They might even cut themselves and do other types of self-injury. These people are not bad people, but they surely are not taking care of their bodies. If you struggle with any of these problems or addictions now or down the road, you will want to get help. Honoring God with your body is a most important step in living out the Purity Code.

Renewing Your Mind for the Good

"Do not conform any longer to the pattern of this world, but be transformed by the renewing of your mind. Then you will be able to test and approve what God's will is—his good, pleasing and perfect will." (Romans 12:2). Your imagination and ability to think make your mind your most powerful sex organ! How you fill your mind determines so much about the quality and purity of your life. No matter what age, if you learn to starve your mind of bad stuff and instead feed it good things, then, as the Scripture in Romans says, you can live by God's good and perfect will.

The following story delivers a good lesson: A man met with a counselor to talk about a dream he kept having about a white cat fighting a black cat. The counselor asked, "Well, who wins the fight?" The man answered, "Whichever cat I feed the most." This is similar to renewing your mind. If you put good things into your mind, good things will win out. The Bible even says peace will come: *"Whatever is true, whatever is noble, whatever is right, whatever is pure, whatever is lovely, whatever is admirable—if anything is excellent or praiseworthy—think* about such things . . . *and the God of peace will be with you"* (Philippians 4: 8–9, emphasis mine). The opposite happens when you "feed on" bad things. In chapter 5, you will learn more about this idea of "garbage in/garbage out."

All of this is why I challenge you to spend time each day, even just a few minutes, reading a devotional or section of Scripture. I challenge you to listen to good music that will lift you up and keep your mind set on positive things. It is also important to find friends who will provide you with healthy conversation. In other words, do stuff that keeps your mind focused on the good.

When we focus our minds on bad stuff, that's when we find ourselves getting into trouble. If you watch, listen to, and read things that lack purity, guess what will happen? Eventually what you put in your mind will come out in actions. Just this week I was talking with a student who said he was having a real problem with using bad language. I asked one question: "Are you willing to quit watching media that constantly goes in that bad-language direction?" I knew this person to be an avid watcher of films and TV that tend to be on the crude side of life. If he was ever going to see change, this person needed to make a decision about what he was putting inside his life. The secret is to *"set your minds on the things above, and not on earthly things"* (Colossians 3:2).

Turning Your Eyes From Worthless Things

"Your eye is a lamp that provides light for your body. When your eye is good, your whole body is filled with light" (Matthew 6:22 NLT). These words of Jesus might be the inspiration for the saying, "Your eyes are a window to your soul." But did you know that your eyes are also a window to your brain? Your brain basically takes a picture of everything you see and stores it in your mind.

The secret is to protect your eyes from bad stuff. Unfortunately, there's bad stuff almost everywhere. Just think about what you've seen on TV, in movies, or even in person. Do an experiment. Close your eyes and picture whatever is in your mind. I'm guessing you had no problem seeing an image or scene that was not very pure.

I live at the coast in Southern California, and I am an avid beach guy. From an early age, I have worn sunglasses to protect my eyes from the sun. In many ways, in order to live by the Code, you will have to learn to protect your eyes from unhealthy sights that can creep into your mind—sights that can take you down a negative road. One key piece of advice is to "bounce your eyes," an idea that comes from my friend Steve Arterburn and his coauthor, Fred Stoeker. It's natural to notice sexual images, but look away as soon as possible (bounce your eyes) so you don't stare. This gives your mind less time to take a picture—a picture that can never be deleted.

I recently told a group of students, "I wouldn't want to be your age today." They looked at me with curiosity. "The temptations you face, things like pornography, are potentially more than I could have handled at your age."

In chapter 8 we'll talk more about pornography (sexual photos and videos), but for now, just know that people who want to live by the Code turn their eyes from worthless things. By far it is the best way to live life to the fullest.

Guarding Your Heart Above All Else

"Guard your heart above all else, for it determines the course of your life" (Proverbs 4:23 NLT). This proverb summarizes pretty well how to live by the Purity Code. We have to guard our hearts.

I was talking recently to a young man who really let his life slip. He was from a strong Christian family and grew up learning the Purity Code. When he got to college, he let his guard down, though, and allowed negative Internet use, alcohol and drugs, and a lack of commitment to God take over his life. His life is pretty messed up now. He told me, "The whole time I knew what I was allowing to enter my heart, but I just didn't care." I am hoping he is on his way back toward living a good and pure life, but he is going to have to carry some negative baggage into adulthood.

My hope for you is that you will feed your heart with good and guard against the negative stuff the world will try to throw at you. Frankly, I don't know how a young person can do it without constantly seeking God's strength and God's will.

There is no better time than right now to make the Purity Code your prayer of commitment to God. You don't have to fully understand every aspect of it, and you will not do it perfectly. After all, you are a human being who at times stumbles like everyone else. But as you move through this very important book and message, my challenge to you is to open up your heart to all that God has for you. Before you turn to the next chapter, offer the Purity Code as your prayer to God.

In honor of God, my family, and my future spouse, I commit my life to sexual purity.

If you prayed that prayer today, then mark down the date. (There's also a page at the end of this book to sign a purity pledge, or you can make a printout at *www.homeword.com*.) It will end up being one of the most important sentences you have ever prayed to God. If you weren't ready to pray the prayer, that's okay. Keep reading and deciding. The decisions you make as you investigate the Code can affect you for your life now and in eternity.

Discussion Starters

1. Brainstorm positive results of following the Purity Code.
2. What are some of the negative consequences of not committing to the Code?
3. Which of the four ways to follow the Code do you think is most challenging?
   * Honoring God with your **body**
   * Renewing your **mind** for the good
   * Turning your **eyes** from worthless things
   * Guarding your **heart** above all else
4. Do you think you are ready to commit to the Code?

CHAPTER TWO

The Foundation:
Developing a Healthy Sexuality

To fully live according to the Purity Code, you will need to develop a healthy view of sex and sexuality. That's what this chapter is about, but first a warning: the information here is blunt and straightforward. For some of you, this may be the most you've ever learned about the subject! I've spent most of my adult years talking to students about sex, and after twenty-five years of listening to students ask about sex and telling me their stories, I have a few important conclusions I want to share with you.

First of all, some teens and preteens make unhealthy sexual decisions based primarily on three factors:

- Peer pressure
- Emotional involvement that exceeds their maturity level
- Lack of healthy, positive, Christian sex education

Another factor is what a person thinks of himself or herself. Show me someone who is sexually promiscuous, and I'll bet they are struggling with a poor self-image. Here is part of a letter I received from a student in Florida:

> *I'm not a bad person. I'm not the best-looking person in the world, but I'm not the worst. I have an okay personality. For the last two years I've had sex with five different boyfriends. I don't know why I always let them have their way, but I do. I guess I want them to like me, and I'm afraid if I don't let them try things [sexually], then they won't want me as a girlfriend.*

This girl means well—she wants to be liked, but she is not making good decisions. Her self-image isn't very good, and she lacks a healthy view of her sexuality. This is why I am so adamant about putting the Purity Code in front of your generation. You may be growing up in the most difficult culture *ever* to follow the Code.

One big challenge is the mixed messages many of you get about sex. Have you heard any of the following?

- Parents say, "Don't do it . . ." (and then nothing else is discussed—silence).
- The church says, "Don't do it because it's sinful . . ." (and then . . . silence).
- The school teaches, "This is how you do it . . ." (but doesn't discuss morality or values).
- Some musicians and actors say, "Sex is great . . . just make sure you protect yourself."
- When you are older, some of your friends may say, "I do it and

it's great!" (when perhaps they really don't do it—or it's not always so great).

Most students don't receive thorough, positive sex education at home. If you *can* talk to your parents about sex, you are fortunate—not many kids do. Parents often are not confident about teaching about sex or know how to bring it up. It can be even more difficult to talk about healthy sexuality because your sexuality is more than what you do with your body. Sexuality involves your feelings and attitudes for yourself, as well as how you feel and act toward others. If your parents bought you this book and are willing to discuss sex and sexuality, they deserve praise! Only recently has the church begun talking about a healthy view of sexuality. With a culture so preoccupied with sex, this important subject must be discussed.

Unfortunately, most schools that offer family-life or sex-education programs provide what I call "value-neutral education." In other words, these programs talk about things like birth control and sexual techniques, but they don't offer any values or moral perspective.

If someone from another planet visited earth, they would think we worship sex because so much of what we see and hear in the media is related to sex. You might even find that friends or acquaintances, because of their own lack of healthy sexuality, will "brag" about sexual experiences, whether they really occurred or not. It is easy to wrongly think that everyone is having sex.

Sex

If you have a pulse, you *will* eventually think about sex. In fact, it's quite natural at your age (or any age, for that matter) to have sexual thoughts and questions.

I came across an interesting statistic a few years ago: The average sixteen-year-old male has a sexual thought every twenty seconds. Actually, I have no idea whether it is true, but I shared this information with a group of students in North Carolina. Afterward, a sixteen-year-old guy came up to me and asked, "You know that statistic about having a sexual thought every twenty seconds?" I nodded my head, and he continued, "Well, what am I supposed to think about the other nineteen seconds? It's always on my mind!"

I still don't know if he was serious, but I think you get the point. It's very *common* and *normal* to think about sex.

Sex and sexuality influences all of our lives. Some people think about it more at different ages, but natural curiosity about human sexuality begins pretty early. Before they were five years old, each of my three girls was, in her own innocent way, exploring her sexuality. They didn't have crushes on boys then, but were already learning that boys and girls have different plumbing and fixtures (translation: body parts).

God has created each and every one of us with a sex drive; He wants couples to fall in love, get married, and have children. Besides this God-given sex drive, I can think of at least three other reasons sex will be an important part of your life.

1. Sex Is Everywhere in Our Culture.

One of the main reasons sex influences our lives is that it's *everywhere*. Think of the many songs you've heard containing sexual situations, suggestive imagery, or sexually explicit words. Watch one evening of TV and count all the sexual innuendos. Even the most innocent movies often hint at sex. Every form of media—newspapers, magazines, radio, television, billboards, and, of course, the Internet—uses sex to get our attention. The wisdom of the world says that sex sells.

In my neighborhood there is a billboard that shows two images: a bottle of alcohol and the bare back of a woman who is looking over her shoulder. I have no idea what the correlation is between a woman's body and the company's product. I couldn't even begin to tell you what the bottle looks like, but I can describe that woman's back in detail!

Last year, prime-time TV aired more than fourteen thousand acts of sexual intercourse or hints of intercourse. (*Intercourse* is discussed more in chapter 3, but for now, it can briefly be described as when a man puts his penis inside a woman's vagina.) But it doesn't just occur on prime-time TV; daytime soap operas and similar shows are also filled with sex. Did you know that on the "soaps," 94 percent of all acts or hints of sex involve people not married to each other? Need I say more? Sex is everywhere in our culture, and it can't help but have an influence in our lives.

2. Sex Is Mysterious.

A few summers ago, Cathy and I went with our friends Steve and Andrea to the beach (without our kids). We were having a wonderful day when suddenly I started picking up on the conversation of some teenage girls nearby. The girls, who looked so young and innocent, were talking quite loudly about sexual experiences.

For half an hour I listened in, and yes, I was being nosy. Cathy appeared to be sleeping, Andrea was staring out at the ocean, and Steve was reading a magazine. I happened to notice, though, that he never turned a page the entire time! We were *all* listening. Why? Because no matter what your age, sex is mysterious. We're naturally curious about it. I've been married for more than twenty-five years, and I'm still learning about aspects of my sexuality. I think God made sex mysterious because He wanted us to keep it special.

3. Sex Is Enjoyable.

Hearing a guy who challenges people to live by the Purity Code say that sex is enjoyable may be a bit confusing. It is the truth though. Sex can be fun. But I firmly believe God wants the best for you, and that is why He makes it clear in the Bible that we are to save sexual intercourse for marriage. Here, however, we are looking at why sex has such an influence in our lives, and one of the major reasons is that it's usually enjoyable. If it wasn't a very special feeling and experience, it wouldn't be such a big deal.

The reason I tell you sex is fun—and risk possible criticism from your parents—is that I don't want to lie to you. Sex *is* fun. (Of course, I'm not talking here about sexual abuse; "fun" is the last word those who have been subjected to that horrible experience would use.)

Studies tell us that at least 50 percent of Americans will have sexual intercourse by the time they are eighteen years old.[1] Here are some other important statistics about sex and the American teenager. These stats are shocking, but it is my sincere hope that you will choose a better way and go against the grain of the culture.

- Eighty-one percent of today's unmarried males and 67 percent of today's unmarried females had sexual intercourse before the age of twenty.
- There are over four million pornographic Web sites. Ninety percent of eight- to sixteen-year-olds have viewed pornography online (most while doing their homework).

- Twenty-eight percent of fifteen- to seventeen-year-old males have given oral sex to a female. Forty percent of fifteen- to seventeen-year-old males have received oral sex from a female.[2] (We'll talk more about oral sex in chapter 9.)

The good news is that thousands of people are, in a very real sense, rebelling against popular culture and instead making the Purity Code a lifestyle choice. The majority who commit to the Code have a healthy biblical view of sexuality. Unfortunately, many others don't know that the Bible talks quite freely about healthy sexuality and gives us the guidelines to live by.

What Does the Bible Say?

Recently, a teenage couple sat in my office. They had already been sexually active. She wanted to stop their physical relationship but not break up, and he didn't want to stop anything. At the end of our time together, he looked up at me with a real sense of frustration and said, "Is God a grinch when it comes to sex?"

I'm afraid too many people believe that statement to be true when, in fact, it couldn't be further from the truth. Don't forget, sex was God's idea. In Genesis we read that after God created man and woman—and their sexuality—He looked at what He had made and said that it was "very good." God is no grinch when it comes to sex. He created sex and sees it as *very good.*

Some people don't think the Bible has much to say about how we should live out our sexuality. These people haven't done their homework. The Bible is not a sex manual, but it contains several extremely important pieces of wisdom for those who truly desire to be all God wants them to be. Let's take a quick look at a few of the key verses.

The Bible on Adultery

You are probably familiar with the commandment *"you shall not commit adultery"* (Exodus 20:14). Adultery occurs when two people have sexual intercourse and at least one of them is married to someone else. You don't need to be an A student to realize God knew what He was doing when He included this commandment in His "Big Ten." Most people today have seen lives ruined because of an adulterous affair. I can think of entire families whose lives have been radically changed and deeply hurt because of adultery. God wants the best for you. He wants to protect you from the pain of a broken relationship. He has established this rule for a good reason.

The Bible on Fornication

Paul wrote, *"It is God's will that you should be sanctified: that you should avoid sexual immorality"* (1 Thessalonians 4:3). Here's a quick Greek lesson: The original word for "immorality" in this verse is *pornea.* It's where we get the root word for pornography or fornication. Some Bible translations even use the word *fornication* instead of *immorality.* Fornication occurs when two people who are not married have sex. Again, is God trying to mess up our fun? No way. He knows what's best for us. He loves us. He deeply understands the confusion and heartache caused by those who choose to go against His will. I wish you could hear the stories about broken relationships from kids I met who have broken the Code. There is guilt, pain, confusion, and, for some, a feeling of hopelessness. Again, God surely knew what He was doing when he came up with the command to refrain from sex until marriage.

The Bible on the Union Between Man and Wife: One Flesh

" 'Haven't you read,' [Jesus] replied, 'that at the beginning the Creator "made them male and female," and said, "For this reason a man will leave his father and mother and be united to his wife, and the two will become one flesh"? So, they are no longer two, but one. Therefore what God has joined together, let man not separate' " (Matthew 19:4–6). As this Scripture shows, God sees a physical sexual relationship as very sacred and special. Sex is physical, but it is also a spiritual union. The words "casual sex" are not in His vocabulary.

There is no better example of being united as *one flesh* than when a man and woman have sexual intercourse. Sexual intercourse is as intimate as you can get. Are you prepared to become one flesh with another person? It's a very serious consideration to make *before* you find yourself in a compromising situation. There is just no such thing as casual sex, even though movies, music, and things on the Internet sometimes try to make it look that way.

The Bible on the Human Body

As a Christian, there is absolutely no doubt that your very own body is a temple of God: *"Flee from sexual immorality. All other sins a man commits are outside his body, but he who sins sexually sins against his own body. Do you not know that your body is a temple of the Holy Spirit, who is in you, whom you have received from God? You are not your own; you were bought at a price. Therefore honor God with your body"* (1 Corinthians 6:18–20). I'm not a theologian, but I do know that in a mysterious way, God's Holy Spirit lives within each Christian believer. Our body should glorify and honor God; after all; He created us and lives inside us. And, as you read in the previous chapter, a major part of the Purity Code is honoring God with our bodies.

Many other verses in Scripture focus on the subject of sex and sexuality other than the ones I've mentioned. It is clear from these, though, that God views our sexuality as very good, very special, and even sacred. He's *not* a grinch! He wants the best for us. That's why He wants us to wait to have sexual intercourse until we are married. Sex is much more than sexual intercourse, however, and my belief is that it is nearly impossible to be loose on other purity issues and still abstain from sexual intercourse until marriage.

So the foundation for a healthy sexuality comes from one source: the Bible. The decision is yours: to follow the wisdom of God, or to go with the modern culture. I think you would agree with me that God's way is the right way. It is not the easy way. You will be tempted. You will most likely accidentally view pornography on the Internet. You will have strong desires to compromise the Purity Code, but the Creator of sexuality can also give you the strength and discipline to follow His Code.

Discussion Starters

1. List areas of our culture that present sexuality in ways that are opposite of the Purity Code.
2. What do you think makes our sexuality so incredibly special and unique?
3. What did you learn about developing a healthy sexuality from the Bible verses and thoughts in this chapter?
4. Do the scriptures and points about healthy sexuality make sense to you? Why or why not?

YOUR BODY

CHAPTER THREE

Changes in Your Body

Your body is ever changing. From the day you were conceived until right now, things have been changing, growing, dying, all in constant movement. But when it comes to sexuality, there is a "Big Time" of change: puberty.

Puberty usually happens between the ages of ten-and-a-half and fourteen. Some bodies change earlier and some later. I had hair underneath my arms in fourth grade, and one kid I knew got one little hair on his chest at age sixteen. Some girls fill out sooner than most, and others are late bloomers. One thing about the human body is that basically it all works out in the end! The timing on when all the body changes happen is really no big deal, but when you're in the midst of them, it is very important to understand some of these changes. It is normal to have curiosity, and it is normal to have questions.

This chapter has the chance of being a bit embarrassing, but we still need to have this talk. Everybody eventually has to talk about this stuff, so it might as well be now.

I mentioned that I have three daughters. Each reacted differently to this information when she was around your age. One of them was totally into it. She asked many questions. The conversation was engaging and encouraging. The next one listened quietly. Her eyes were as big as saucers. She didn't have any questions and wanted to move on to the next subject as quickly as possible. Our youngest daughter informed us that she already knew this stuff because her sisters had explained everything in detail to her—with drawings!

There is no right way to react. But the information is important, even if some of the drawings are a bit embarrassing. (Sorry.)

Guys and Girls Are Created Differently

Physically and emotionally, things are changing pretty rapidly. Your body and your mind are going through some major changes and growth spurts. Some of the changes that guys and gals experience are very similar, but guys and girls do approach sexuality and relationships very differently. That is why your commitment to the Purity Code is extremely important at this stage of your life.

Just last night as I was coming home from work, I noticed a neighbor girl hugging and kissing a guy at the park near our house. Only three months ago we were at her house and she told me she wasn't interested in boys yet. I couldn't help notice that her body was "in transition" of becoming a young woman. Today, she is in a different body with a different mindset. I hope she is ready!

My pastor always used to say, "God is never too early, and He is never too late." Whether someone is excited or not about puberty, it shows up right on schedule for each person. We just have to make sure we are knowledgeable and ready for those changes. The changes are unique for each person, but basic things will happen to your body and emotions that are similar to your friends'. As we look at these changes and differences between guys and girls, make sure you are aware that the Master Designer has created every detail of your body, and He plays a vital role in every aspect of its development. From the day you were just an embryo in your mother's womb, God was looking out for you. And as you read this chapter, keep in mind what David said in the book of Psalms: *"For you created my inmost being; you knit me together in my mother's womb. I praise you because I am fearfully and wonderfully made; your works are wonderful, I know that full well. My frame was not hidden from you when I was made in the secret place. When I was woven together in the depths of the earth, your eyes saw my unformed body"* (Psalm 139:13–16).

Emotional Changes

Guys, you're first. Some guys develop later than many girls emotionally and even sexually. When I was twelve, I was still really short and had a semi-crush on Sue Stonestreet, who was really tall. We were the same age, but she had already grown and developed into a young woman while I still had a squeaky voice and stood about six inches shorter than her. She saw me as a squirrelly, awkward boy, so she obviously had no interest in me! But hey, I could still dream.

Guys your age are very physical. Many of you like to wrestle around with your friends. Actually, you are craving physical intimacy. You are physical with your eyes and even with your hands. Guys in general have an easier time disconnecting their body from their mind, heart, and soul. Believe me, this can get you into trouble. In fact, when it comes

39

to sexuality, guys will often give love to get sex. They are stimulated by what their eyes see, and they want it!

Girls are more emotional. Many girls going through puberty have a great deal of drama over relationships. Relationships with their girl friends as well as with guys are a natural part of their life. They crave emotional intimacy. Their body, unlike some of their guy friends', is extremely connected to their mind, heart, and soul. Girls too often give sex to get love. That's just the opposite of their male counterparts. Girls today can be visually stimulated like guys, but they are much more moved through words, tender touch, and romance—in other words, their emotions.

Women are excited sexually by what they hear, and men are excited by what they see. Is either way wrong? Not necessarily. They are just different. The earlier you understand the difference, the better off you will be in living out the Purity Code.

When I talked with my daughters about modesty issues and clothing choices, I related it to guys being more aroused through their eyes. They had a hard time understanding where I was coming from. After all, they were girls and they didn't get us guys. At the same time, when I talk with guys about girls and their need for emotional involvement, I might as well be talking a foreign language to them. It reminds me of a book that came out a few years ago called *Men Are From Mars, Women Are From Venus*. That title is a good illustration of how guys and girls are so extremely different. In order to live out the Purity Code, you will have to understand at least a bit of the differences, or you may find yourself having problems with the opposite sex. Don't think you will ever totally figure out the differences, though. I have been married to Cathy for over twenty-five years, and believe me, I am still in the dark on some subjects!

Physical Differences

Okay, this time the girls go first, and this is where I promised those drawings!

Girls: Your Sexual System

As I have studied the human body systems and especially the sexual systems, I am amazed at how the Master Designer of our bodies thought of everything. The entire system was created with you and me in mind. It is beautiful, intricate, practical (!), and even in many situations, enjoyable.

I have a very good friend who is a gynecologist, and she tells me that a majority of girls really don't understand their sexual systems when they come in to visit her for the first time. She also says that most men she has met in the course of delivering thousands of babies not only have no clue about the female sexual system, they don't understand their own either! So here is an explanation of the sexual systems—females first. I do want to mention, though, that there are other books available for a much more detailed look at the physiological and biological particulars of most of the important parts of female and male bodies. I'm the guy who had to take biology class twice to actually understand it! Of course, this gives your parents a great amount of confidence in me for this chapter!

One of the first visual changes in a young woman's body is a growth in breast size and broadening of the hips. Before puberty, a girl's and guy's chest looks much the same. No matter the size, breasts have two parts: *milk glands* that connect to the nipples through tiny tubes, and *fatty tissues* that make the breasts soft. As much as our modern culture focuses on the size of breasts, God's plan was to produce a very efficient way to feed a baby. A female's hips will

BECOMING **A WOMAN**

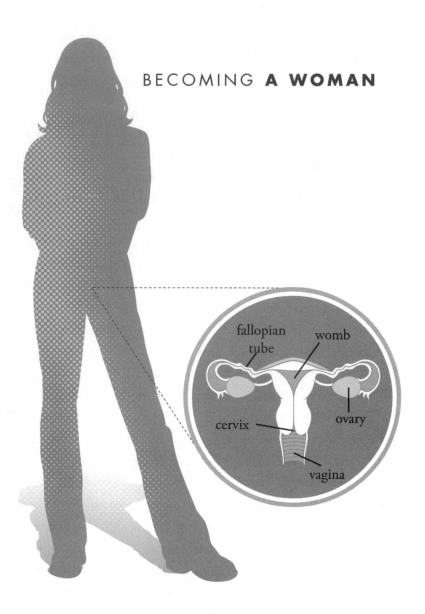

fallopian tube

womb

cervix

ovary

vagina

typically broaden and hair begins to grow in the pubic area (the front part of the body that your underwear covers) and under the arms. All this is natural and oftentimes welcomed by young girls.

A woman has a pair of *ovaries* that begin to come alive in a different way at puberty. There are thousands of underdeveloped *egg cells* stored in the ovaries, and somewhere between the ages of ten and thirteen, the ovaries begin to produce *estrogen*. This hormone helps control the many changes going on inside your body. Approximately once a month, after puberty, the ovaries release an egg. This is called *ovulation*. The egg moves into the *Fallopian tubes*, which connect the ovaries with the uterus. The Fallopian tubes have the important job of being the pathway your egg travels to the womb. They are also the place where the male sperm and female egg meet to create a baby. (More on that in a moment.) The *uterus* is also called the womb, and that is where a baby grows until birth. When an egg is not fertilized (no sperm is present to fertilize the egg), then it moves on down to the uterus and eventually through the blood lining of the uterus, and you have your period.

The *vagina* is a passageway that during birth becomes the birth canal. It is a three- to four-inch tube made of elastic muscle. During sexual intercourse, the vagina expands and lubricates itself to make intercourse easier and more pleasurable. As you can sense, everything has a purpose and is connected in one way or another. The vagina is connected to the *cervix*, which is a strong muscle that separates the vagina from the uterus. The main job of a cervix is to create somewhat of a mucous plug when a woman gets pregnant to protect the fluid sac around the baby in the womb. Are you confused yet?

The next part of the sexual system is connected to the vagina. Next to the vaginal opening is the *urethra*. The urethra is located in front of and totally separate from the vaginal canal, and it is the passageway that allows urine to exit the body. The *labia* are two different sets of skin folds to protect the vagina. The *clitoris* is a very small organ located toward the front of a woman's vagina with tissue that functions as a pleasurable nerve ending for sexual excitement. Frankly, God thought of everything; He even cares about enjoyment in marital sexuality.

Okay, on to the guys, and then back to reproduction.

Typically, the first outward sign for a young man who is beginning the journey of puberty is that *hair* will begin to grow above the penis. Since all people develop at different ages and stages, the guys' locker room can be a bit intimidating because some guys will have hair and some will not. The next thing that happens is the *penis* and *scrotum* will have a growth spurt. Just like breasts, penises are different sizes for everyone.

The penis is made up of soft tissue, and it basically has three parts. The *shaft* is the longer part and is connected to the head or *glans.* The glans has very smooth and sensitive skin that is a bit different from the shaft of the penis. There is a hole at the end of the glans where the man passes urine and sperm. We will get to the sperm in a minute. The other part of the penis is what is called the *foreskin.* The foreskin is a continuation of the skin on the shaft that covers the glans. Some guys get the foreskin cut off at just a few days old. This is called *circumcision.* Jewish boys and a majority of American boys are circumcised. Other cultures do not tend to be circumcised. With modern medicine today, it is a matter of parental choice more than anything else.

Hanging below the penis is a sac-like part of a man's body called the *scrotum.* The scrotum houses two key parts of the male sexual system called testes or testicles. They are two small egg-shaped organs that have two very important functions: The testicles produce *testosterone,* which is the hormone that keeps guys looking like guys and produces the beard and other male features. The other function of the testicles is the production of *sperm,* which is needed to fertilize a woman's egg and create a child. As young men reach puberty, their testicles begin

BECOMING **A MAN**

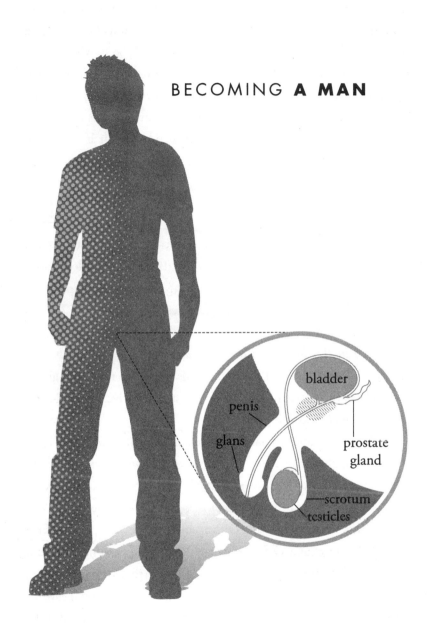

bladder

penis

glans

prostate
gland

scrotum

testicles

to produce about 100 million sperm every day. The testosterone in a man's body helps the *prostate gland* and other glands produce fluid that mixes with the sperm to come out of a man's body when he has an *ejaculation*, which is the process during sexual stimulation when a male's penis becomes firm and ejaculates *semen*. Semen is a white milky substance that is a mixture of sperm and other fluids from those male glands. When your birth dad's sperm and your birth mom's egg met after sexual intercourse, you came into existence!

Pregnancy

Okay, let's get this straight: You were not delivered to your parents by a stork! No, as I mentioned earlier, the Bible is quite clear about human sexuality. At most Christian wedding ceremonies, a Scripture is read to the couple. It is found in the Old Testament, and Jesus quoted it in the New Testament. He said, *"For this reason a man will leave his father and mother and be united to his wife, and the two will become one flesh"* (Matthew 19:5). Although this Scripture is talking about much more than sexual intercourse, it is a descriptive illustration of two individuals becoming one.

When a man and woman experience sexual intercourse, two bodies have literally become one. In a loving marriage, the experience of sexual intercourse should be a wonderful feeling of bringing two who have committed their lives together to become one. The feeling can be euphoric with enjoyment. During intercourse, the penis is firm and inside the vagina. When ejaculated, between two hundred and six hundred million sperm are released inside the woman's vagina. Although this is a simplified description, imagine the sperm "swimming" like fish through the vaginal canal, cervix, and uterus into the Fallopian tube where, at a certain time of the month, the woman's egg will greet the sperm that made it through this long journey. (The vast amount of sperm die before getting to the Fallopian tubes.) The sperm and egg unite, and presto, the sperm fertilizes the egg. At this amazingly miraculous moment a baby is conceived.[1]

Personally, I believe that when an egg is fertilized, not only is it one of the most remarkable miracles of God, but that fertilized egg is also the beginning of a baby's life. Shown here are illustrations of what is taking place in the life of a baby while in the mother's womb. Yes, a baby can look rather strange in the first two months—almost E.T.-like—but the amazing part is that by week four or five, the heart is already beating with a regular rhythm.

3.5 weeks

7.5 weeks

10 weeks

12 weeks

24 weeks

Masturbation

Now, before I let you move on from this already embarrassing chapter, there is one other topic I want to discuss, and that is masturbation. Studies say that masturbation is pretty much a universal experience. Masturbation is technically called "auto-eroticism." Auto means "self" and eroticism means "sexual stimulation." Basically, masturbation is "self-sexual stimulation." Even for small children, it is quite normal for them to explore their body parts. This is not something that is dirty or evil but rather is normal and should be expected.

As young people reach puberty and their bodies are changing, self-exploration sometimes becomes sexual or sensual. More guys than girls encounter a masturbation experience, but girls definitely do experience it as well. There are silly myths about masturbation that say if you do it you might go blind or start growing hair on your knuckles. Those are obviously just ridiculous rumors, but you would be amazed at how many people actually believe stuff like that.

Now, since the main focus of this book is living out the Purity Code, let's see how masturbation relates to purity.

Masturbation and the Purity Code

Interestingly enough, the Bible does not speak to the exact issue of masturbation. The Bible does, however, deal with lust, fantasy, and faithfulness to our spouse or future spouse. Again, even though masturbation is normal, there are some concerns. Jesus said, " *'Do not commit adultery.' But I tell you that anyone who looks at a woman lustfully has already committed adultery with her in his heart"* (Matthew 5:27–28). This verse sets very high standards for the Purity Code. (By the way, just because Jesus talked about males who lust after females, the same applies to females looking at males lustfully.) Basically, Jesus is saying that if you or I entertain thoughts of lust toward someone, we have broken one of the Ten Commandments. Many people would argue that you can't have a masturbation experience without feeling lust. In addition, many people even go so far as to say that masturbation did not satisfy their lustful or sexual desires, but instead fueled the fire for more lustful thoughts.

One day while speaking to several thousand students about the Purity Code, a young woman asked if she could speak to me privately. She was very concerned that she practiced masturbation regularly and often did it after she got in a fight with her mother. She was using masturbation as a way to cope with stress. This can become what is known as obsessive-compulsive behavior. Other times, guys have told me that they have a masturbation experience daily or several times a day. This, too, is not healthy because of the obsessive-compulsive nature of the experience. Far too many people use masturbation as a sexual release while observing pornography on the Internet. This involves lust, fantasy, and a false type of intimacy. If you find yourself in any of these kinds of situations, seek help. Of course it is a bit embarrassing to tell someone about this kind of a problem or to ask questions about it, but believe me, a counselor or pastor has heard it all.

My friend Shannon Ethridge, a best-selling author and advocate of healthy sexuality, told me in an interview on my radio program, "The only way to kill a bad habit is to starve it." I believe that when we live by the Purity Code, we will also have to deal with the negative side to the habit of masturbation. Lust, fantasy, and obsessive-compulsive behaviors keep our minds, hearts, bodies, and eyes away from purity and focused on things that can take us down the wrong road. However, we can overcome poor habits by focusing on what is good and right.

As your body changes it will be important to have the courage to ask questions and share with trusted people your questions and concerns about all areas of your sexuality. To overcome a poor masturbation habit, you may need to find someone you trust to confess your concerns to if you fall to temptation. You may need counseling to understand why you do what you do. Remember, though, that sex was created by God for good. We want to experience all the blessings and freedom of a life of purity. No one said it would be easy. But there is a way that leads to joy and freedom. It's the way of the Code.

Discussion Starters

1. What makes puberty exciting? A bit scary?
2. What did you learn in this chapter that is new to you? (For parents and students!)
3. What part of this chapter is most helpful? Which part is most uncomfortable to talk about?
4. Pregnancy is an incredible miracle of God. Any ideas on why God would use sexuality as such an important part in the creation of babies?

CHAPTER FOUR

Is Sex Safe?

At your age you may be thinking, *I'm still not sure what the big deal is about sex. Why does everyone talk about it, sing about it, write about it, and make entire movies about it?* One reason might be the long history sex has.

Just today I reread the creation account in the Bible and was again reminded that sex is God's idea. It says straight out that Adam and Eve had sexual intercourse. (*"Adam lay with his wife Eve, and she became pregnant . . ."* Genesis 4:1.) Our sexuality is definitely meant to be safe, special, and intimate between a husband and wife, and it is one of the most incredible experiences in life. However, when someone breaks the Code, sex isn't safe.

So far we have primarily focused on the healthy and positive aspects of living by the Purity Code, but this chapter looks at some of the negative results of not living by the Code.

Yes, as beautiful as your sexuality is, it can be unsafe not only for your body, but also for your emotions, mind, and spirit. Remember the Code is about guarding your mind, body, eyes, and heart. It all goes together.

Physical Consequences

Julie and Ted were only sixteen when they got carried away at a party and had sexual intercourse. Julie was so wrapped up emotionally with Ted that even though she wanted to say no, she was afraid to tell him to stop. They had previously made a commitment to purity, but they let their guard down that night and compromised their values. It had not entered their minds to use birth control because they had not planned on "going all the way." It just sort of happened.

Several weeks later, Julie learned she was pregnant. When she told Ted, he was hardly understanding or supportive. Julie felt alone and used. (More on their story in just a moment.)

Recent studies show that the vast majority of guys and girls who had sex outside of marriage wish they would have waited. Sexual intercourse doesn't automatically lead to pregnancy, but many young people are taking a chance for a few moments of ecstasy with someone they probably aren't going to marry. Pregnancy changes a person's life in a huge way. All of a sudden the responsibility of raising a child, deciding to marry or not to marry, and all the other issues of pregnancy become a major focus. When God said, "Refrain from sexual immorality," He absolutely knew what He was doing.

Now, let's talk openly and honestly about pregnancy. If you are a guy, you bear the same responsibility as the pregnant woman except you obviously don't carry the baby. Way too many guys ignore their responsibilities when a girl gets pregnant. It's just wrong. A person of integrity will take on the responsibility of the pregnancy. The easy way out is to ignore and avoid, but that is not the right way at all.

One of the biggest decisions a person (hopefully the couple) will make is what to do with the baby. Notice that I used the word "baby." Since it has a heartbeat, I believe it is a live human being, so for me personally, abortion is not an option for couples. Therefore, there are only two options: parent the child themselves or choose another family to parent their child. Both decisions are incredibly courageous, given the fact that about 30 percent of teen pregnancies are ended with abortion.[1] Keeping the baby changes your life forever, and so does adoption. I strongly suggest that the birth mother and the birth father, whenever possible, seek counseling at a pregnancy care center.

I happen to think that any young person who is not ready to raise a child should at least consider adoption. Cathy and I are deeply grateful to a courageous birth mother who had a child without being married and allowed us the privilege of raising our oldest daughter. Cathy and I had been unable to have children because of infertility, and we consider the gift of life that our daughter's birth mother gave to be nothing short of a miracle.

Talking about miracles brings me back to the story of Julie and Ted. Julie was in my youth group when she got pregnant. She knew she wasn't ready to raise a child, so she did the courageous thing and chose the adoption process. Today there is a child who one day will be deeply grateful that Julie and Ted chose not to abort him. Julie and Ted have some pain in their lives because of their poor choice, but they can also rest assured there is a child and a couple who are very grateful to them.

Pregnancy is survivable, but there are other issues surrounding sexual activity that carry lifelong physical and emotional consequences.

Sexually Transmitted Diseases (STDs)

Did you know that choosing to have sexual relations outside of a safe marital relationship is a gamble, almost like playing Russian roulette? Notice I said "sexual relations" rather than sexual intercourse. That's because sexually transmitted diseases are possible with *any* kind of genital contact.

I know a girl who some might say was technically a virgin (she had never had intercourse), but she did have other forms of sexual contact with a boy and was later shocked to find out she had a common STD called the herpes simplex virus. The shock only got worse when her doctor informed her there was no cure for the disease. She would live with it for the rest of her life. She had no idea of the consequences of a sexual activity that she thought was harmless because she wasn't "going all the way." Fortunately, after that she made a lasting commitment to live by the Purity Code and ended up marrying a man who accepted the fact of her disease and the ongoing, costly medicine it would require.

THE FACTS

We need to get some facts straight about sexual activity that occurs outside of marriage. Quite simply, it isn't as safe as the movies make it out to be. Just look at the statistics. Over nineteen million cases of STDs (sometimes called venereal disease or VD) have been reported in each of the last few years, and half of those who contacted an STD were between the ages of fifteen and twenty-four. All of this is putting STDs at an epidemic level. The news gets even worse for those who don't live by the Code. In a recent *Time* magazine cover story on STDs, it was reported that if the epidemic continues, almost all young people who are sexually active will eventually have an STD, in large part because the average sexually active young person has about seven different relationships before age twenty. Plain and simple, the physical consequences of sexual promiscuity are very serious.

Until the 1970s there were only two major types of sexually transmitted diseases: syphilis and gonorrhea. Today there are, at last count, over twenty-five different types of STDs. This chapter isn't intended to be the "answer-all" on STDs, but let me give you some basics on the more well-known forms.

Syphilis and Gonorrhea

Syphilis and gonorrhea are both considered bacterial infections and can be treated with antibiotics such as penicillin. Before penicillin was invented in 1928, though, millions of people died from the diseases. Today, syphilis and gonorrhea can be cured if treated early enough, but because they are associated with sexual promiscuity, people are sometimes embarrassed to get medical exams. Both are transmitted through sexual contact. Some call gonorrhea a "silent disease" because since there aren't always symptoms at first, people can be infected but not know it. If untreated, gonorrhea can cause a person to be sterile (unable to have children) or lead to crippling forms of arthritis, meningitis, and even heart disease. Cures exist for these bacterial diseases, but the way to avoid them in the first place is to live by the Code!

HIV/AIDS

HIV (human immunodeficiency virus) is one of the most well-known viruses in the world. HIV can develop into AIDS (acquired immune deficiency syndrome), which robs the body of its ability to fight off infections and eventually can cause death. HIV and AIDS can be spread through oral and genital intercourse. HIV can even be passed to a newborn if the mother is infected. HIV/AIDS does not have a known cure yet. At first it was thought to be primarily a disease that struck homosexual men (men who have sex with men), but studies show that more heterosexual people are now getting HIV/AIDS than homosexuals.

HPV

Human papillomavirus (HPV) is the most common viral STD in the United States. Because we hear so much about HIV today, a lot of people confuse HPV with HIV, but they are different STDs. There are at least seventy types of HPV, all spread through genital contact. Teachers in sex-education classes often talk about protecting oneself from STDs by using a condom, which is made of a rubber-type material and covers the penis during sex. However, condoms provide very little protection from the HPV virus. There is no medical cure for HPV, and it is the leading reason for all cervical cancers, and it can lead to other types of cancer. If a person gets HPV, they might begin to develop warts on their genitals, but warts can also develop inside a woman's cervix. Sometimes with HPV there are no signs of genital warts, but the virus is still very much alive in the body. Again, another reason to follow the Code!

CHLAMYDIA

This is the most common of the STDs coming from a bacterial infection in the United States. Teenagers have the highest rate of infection with about three million new cases a year. Chlamydia can be treated with antibiotics, but it can lead to a woman becoming sterile. If a person gets chlamydia more than once, the rate of sterility goes up. One of the biggest problems with this STD is that for many men and a majority of women, there are no symptoms, making it another "silent disease" that keeps getting passed around because sexually active people tend to have more than one partner over a period of years.

HERPES 2

Is this beginning to sound like a science class? The last STD I will mention is herpes 2. This disease is also at epidemic levels and is very common in the lives of sexually active young people, in part because it is contracted from *any type* of genital contact, not just intercourse. This might be a surprise to the young people who won't have intercourse but will still have genital contact, because they think they can't get pregnant or get an STD. They may not get pregnant, but most have not even thought about STDs like herpes 2.

Typically, two to twenty-one days after sexual contact with someone who is infected, small painful blisters appear on the genitals. Sometimes a fever also develops. Herpes 2 can be especially dangerous for pregnant women; if the mother experiences a breakout of the blisters at childbirth, it is very possible the newborn could be infected. Again, like some other STDs, there is no known cure for herpes 2.

So much more could be written about STDs. Suffice it to say, sex is not always safe, and there are physical consequences to breaking the Purity Code. It doesn't mean that everyone who doesn't follow the Code will get pregnant or get someone pregnant, and it doesn't mean everyone will develop a sexually transmitted disease, but I think you would agree with me that sexual activity when you're unmarried is a gamble; there are good reasons for living by God's standards. If everyone lived by the Purity Code, there would be no reason for this chapter at all.

Emotional Consequences

Sexual promiscuity doesn't just affect us physically. It may prove to be even more devastating on a person's emotions. Just ask a teenager who gave their body and soul to someone, thinking it was going to be special forever, only to be burned by their partner a short time later.

I have spoken to over a million students on this subject, and while I don't necessarily view myself an expert, I would say that I have heard hundreds and maybe thousands of broken-heart stories. Very few people set out to break the Purity Code, but then a situation comes up and poor judgment sets in. In fact, at this time in your life you may think some of the physical stuff I am describing is kind of gross. But feelings, thoughts, and even actions change when you enter puberty and really start dealing with your sexuality. Emotions play a huge part in this season of life.

I mentioned before that many young people become sexually promiscuous not because they are "bad" kids, but because their emotional involvement exceeds their maturity level and they find themselves in compromising situations. Here is a list of emotions that the students who talk to me feel about their sexual experiences:

- Naughty
- Guilt
- Regret
- Mistrust
- Loss of Respect
- Rejection
- Sadness
- Depression
- Anger

- Loneliness
- Frustration
- Fear
- Worry

Now, those aren't words you hear in the movies or from people who are in a safe, loving, secure marriage. Even so, I am not going to lie to you and say that sexual activity only produces negative feelings. A sense of closeness, joy, and excitement (among other good feelings) are also common. However, far too many young people who were sexually active before marriage now say that they wished they would have waited. Most of them didn't get pregnant or get someone pregnant, and most didn't contract an STD, but they still felt extreme, life-altering emotions. Students who gave in to the temptation of breaking the Code have often told me that it wasn't worth it.

One of my favorite writers and speakers on the subject of teen sexuality is Hayley DiMarco. She says, "A full 25 percent of teenage girls who are sexually active report being depressed all or most of the time."[2] Hayley reported that one study of 8,200 adolescents ages twelve to seventeen found "that those involved in romantic relationships had significantly higher levels of depression than those not involved in romantic relationships."[3] Believe me, there are some pretty great kids who have broken the Code and now are grieving their loss. It doesn't mean they can't find spiritual forgiveness and grace through their decision to seek God's love and forgiveness, but it does mean there could be consequences long after they experience forgiveness.

If I could summarize what I want you to get out of this chapter as it relates to the Purity Code, it is that only sex experienced according to God's design with a loving, secure, safe marriage partner can bring you intimacy, unconditional love, and security. Every decision in life can bring about good or bad consequences, and living by the Code has only positive consequences. The other way is much more of a gamble.

Discussion Starters

1. List the physical consequences of sexual contact outside of marriage.
2. How do you think the emotional consequences of poor choices about sexual contact could affect your life?
3. If you had a friend in school who came to you for advice about becoming sexually involved with a boyfriend or girlfriend, what advice would you give them? Why?
4. If a person lives by the Purity Code, what are some of the ways they will have fewer problems in their life and even in their marriage?

YOUR MIND

CHAPTER FIVE

The Battle for Your Mind

Many years ago, a man was traveling across the country by sneaking from one freight train to the next. One night he climbed into what he thought was an ordinary boxcar and closed the door. It automatically locked shut and trapped him inside. When his eyes adjusted to the light, he realized he was actually inside a refrigerated boxcar and quickly became aware of the intense, freezing cold. He undoubtedly called for help and pounded on the door, but he couldn't get anyone's attention. After many hours of struggle, he lay down on the floor of the railroad car.

As he tried to fight against the freezing cold, he scratched a message on the floor explaining his unfortunate, imminent death. Late the next day, repairmen from the railroad opened the door and found the dead man inside. Though the man looked like he had frozen to death, the truth was the repairmen had come to fix the broken refrigerator unit in that car. Most likely the temperature of the railroad car had never fallen below fifty degrees during the night. The man died because he *thought* he was freezing to death.

Variations of this story have been published in different places, so I'm not sure if it's entirely true, but there's no doubt that the mind is a very powerful thing. In fact, your thoughts have a major influence in nearly everything that happens in your life. The Bible says, *"As he [a man] thinks in his heart, so is he"* (Proverbs 23:7 NKJV). The philosopher Ralph Waldo Emerson wrote, "Man becomes what he thinks about all day long."

You will find that your mind is your most important sex organ. And what you think about will determine if you "win" or "lose" the Purity Code. As I briefly mentioned in chapter 1, if you put garbage into your mind, garbage will come out. If you put good things into your mind, good things will come out. Life is an echo: you get back what you put into it. If you plant negative thoughts and images, what do you suppose will grow inside your mind? So, to live by the Code and have a positive, healthy lifestyle, one major area of your life you will want to work on is what you allow to enter your mind.

Because of our sex-obsessed culture, it is very easy to slip into thinking about sexuality in a negative, unhealthy way. I remember a time when I was watching a PG-13 movie with my wife. In the movie, the hero was married to an evil, bitter woman. As the movie progressed, he met a sweet, kind woman, and I was hoping he would dump his wife and go with the other woman. I actually found myself cheering for adultery. The man was tempted, but in the end, he stayed true to his morals and remained with his wife. When it was over, it hit me that I was hoping for something that would have broken one of the Ten Commandments. How easy it is to go in the wrong direction with our minds and compromise our values if we let our thoughts go in any direction other than purity.

Powerful Influences

You are living in a world with more negative images to fill your mind than any generation before you. If you do not stand firm with what you allow or do not allow into your mind, our society will almost force you to compromise. Don't think for a minute that you are too strong for society.

Even while writing this book, I have been trying to help a struggling college student who was raised in a Christian home. In elementary and middle school, she was a leader in her church and adamant about her quest for purity. She thought she was invincible. Since then, she has walked away from her sexual-purity commitment and struggles with addictions to porn and marijuana. When we looked back at what happened, it was clear that it was not one big thing but rather a bunch of little compromises along the way that helped her stray from her commitments. She lost her discipline. She dropped her guard. She flirted with society, and eventually the negative stuff in her mind pushed her upbringing aside. It started with a poor choice of friends and poor choices of TV, movies, and even magazines. At one time she thought the music she listened to wouldn't cause her to stumble; she had told her mom and dad that she didn't listen to the words. Today, as a college dropout and an addict, she has been humbled. The "it isn't going to happen to me" is not always true. We have to guard our mind and tune out the bad stuff and tune in the good. It will take discipline to keep your mind free of the negative and full of the positive, but discipline is what is needed. Paul gave Timothy some great advice: *"Train yourself to be godly"* (1 Timothy 4:7).

Pornography

We will talk about pornography in greater detail in chapter 8, but it just may be the single thing that will take over the minds of your generation. It is not a force to play with at all. I recently researched pornography's effects on teenagers. Do you realize that more than twelve billion dollars are spent on pornography in America each year? Over half of all American teenagers have at least some exposure to pornography once a month. No wonder so many people have such a struggle with their sexuality.

If you are tempted to look at pornography, even if you think it's out of curiosity, don't do it. When you fill your mind with garbage, the natural tendency is to take it a step further and act upon what you've seen. I've met people who are addicted to pornography, and they would urge you not to even dabble with it. It can start out innocently, but you will develop a hunger for more and more. Absolutely nothing is positive about pornography. I wish they would put up billboards everywhere that read: *Caution: Pornography Is Poison to Your Mind.*

Television

I'm not going to tell you to throw out every TV in your house, but perhaps it's time to think about what comes into your home and into your mind through television. The average student attends school approximately one thousand hours a year; the same student watches more than twelve hundred hours of TV during the same year. And, as mentioned before, fourteen thousand acts of intercourse or sexual innuendos are shown on prime-time TV each year.

If you let your mind focus on too much sexual impurity, it's bound to influence you. Look at how TV commercials can affect your lifestyle and buying habits. Advertisers aren't investing millions of dollars to simply entertain you. They want to sell you products or ideas. You won't be any happier just because you buy a certain pair of jeans or drink the same brand of soft drink a movie star drinks. And when you're older, drinking beer won't make you any funnier or sexier just because the commercials say so.

If we aren't careful, TV soon becomes our reality. The power of the subconscious mind and the influence of television are so powerful that we can forget it is make-believe. A few years ago, more than 250,000 people wrote to a "doctor" on one of the medical TV programs, requesting serious medical advice. This doctor wasn't a real doctor; he only played one on TV! Were all those people crazy? No, they were normal people like you and me who just forgot that TV is fake. If you are a couch potato who is addicted to TV, don't think your problem is innocent. Television has a huge influence on anyone who watches it—no matter the length of time.

Now, let me talk for a moment about reality shows. Do these shows glamorize the Purity Code or destroy it? Just because it's legal to watch doesn't mean it's worth putting that crap into your mind. Yes, I said the word *crap*. Crap is a slang word for feces (poo!), and that is what often gets shoved into our minds, and then we wonder why garbage comes out. My worry is that your generation's morals will slide straight downhill due to the crap that is on television and in all media. I'm not suggesting you throw your TV set away—it is something more difficult. You must learn to tell the difference between the good and the bad, and make godly decisions FOREVER.

Rock Music

You and your friends are probably unified by one common interest more than any other: music. I know that several types of music are popular, including rap, hip-hop, and rock-and-roll, but to simplify things here, I'll categorize it all as rock music. The latest surveys tell us that the average student listens to four hours of rock music per day, and more than 85 percent of young people in the U.S. claim rock (in one form or another) as their favorite kind of music.

Given these kinds of statistics, we must conclude that rock music plays (or will play) a significant role in your life. Even if you do not realize it, your mind is recording *everything* that is placed inside it. In the Christian world, the subject of rock music is very controversial. Some people who have good intentions believe all rock music is literally satanic. Others, who have just as strong convictions, say it's okay to listen to the majority of rock music. But you'll never hear a Christian say that what some call "pornographic rock" is a positive influence for your life. This type of music contains sex-related words or has been made into a video with sexual images.

People frequently ask me where I stand in the rock-and-roll debate. I am personally somewhere between the two extremes. I am deeply concerned about the subtle—and not so subtle—lyrics coming out of the mouths of music superstars. Your mind picks up on the lyrics even when you aren't focusing on the words. The power of the mind is awesome and not to be taken lightly. I have seen hundreds of people lose ground in their relationship with God because their choice of music didn't leave room for their Christian faith. One of the Old Testament writers said, *"Choose for yourselves this day whom you will serve"* (Joshua 24:15). I think lots of teenagers, when faced with that decision, would lean closer to rock-and-roll than to the Rock of our salvation.

On the other hand, just because a song is played on a rock station or has a strong beat, it's not necessarily *evil.* You should be much more concerned with the words than with the beat. I've heard some very raunchy lyrics in some of my parents' slow country-western songs. Basically, you have three options:

1. Don't listen to rock music at all.
2. Constantly listen to rock music.
3. Be a selective listener.

Although many teenagers go with option 2, I hope you won't. Studies of the subconscious mind lead me to believe it's just too dangerous to your lifestyle. Most teens say they don't listen to the lyrics, but when they are asked the words of the songs, even they are surprised at how much of a song they can repeat from memory.

Here are some excellent questions and guidelines for listening to rock music (or any other kind of music):

- Can I glorify Christ by listening to this song?
- Does this song fit within the Purity Code?
- Am I using my time wisely?
- What has control over me?

When you are being totally honest and seeking God's wisdom, these simple questions will help you make the right choices. They will help you intelligently choose what kind of music you will and will not invite into your mind.

Winning the Battle for Your Mind

Media can fool you. Never underestimate the incredible power of music, movies, TV, videos, magazines, and cyberspace; the direct influence they have on your mind is frightening. The garbage in/garbage out principle is the strongest and most sensible principle for dealing with the media. If you feed your mind with negative influences, the negative *will* come out. If you feed it with positive messages, then positive will win. It's really quite simple. What goes in must come out. Because your mind is so much a part of who you are and who you are becoming, let's look at a few practical suggestions for improving your thought life.

Program Your Mind to Think Good Thoughts

Here is a sentence for you to memorize: *I create change in my life when I gain control of my thoughts.* People who live fulfilled lives are in the process of mastering their thought life. Listen to the apostle Paul's sound advice about your thought life:

> *Whatever is true, whatever is noble, whatever is right, whatever is pure, whatever is lovely, whatever is admirable—if anything is excellent or praiseworthy—think about such things. Whatever you have learned or received or heard from me, or seen in me—put it into practice. And the God of peace will be with you.* (Philippians 4:8–9)

Notice what Paul said results from thinking about good things—*peace.* When you plant good thoughts in your life, the roots will grow deep. When the seed of good thoughts begins to sprout, one of its many positive characteristics is peace.

Let me suggest a few ways to prepare yourself to think good thoughts: read and memorize Scripture, choose friends who will build you up, listen to good music, and read inspiring books. In your time of prayer, don't rush it. Take your time praying and thinking. Remember, "As a man thinks in his heart, so is he."

A few years ago, when I needed to keep my focus on the Lord, I decided to read through the entire New Testament. I divided it into ninety sections, approximately three chapters a day. On my appointment calendar, I placed a big mark ninety days from the day I began. Reading the New Testament completely through in a three-month period helped me discipline myself to read for ten to fifteen minutes a day, and it gave me the opportunity to plant good things in my life.

If you truly want to program your mind for good thoughts, find a devotional method that works for you. All of the great men and women of God share one characteristic that stands out above all others: they all had a daily quiet time with God. If you want to think good thoughts and keep your mind focused on God, you must "renew" your mind constantly with good input. Two Scripture verses have been especially helpful to me:

> *You will keep in perfect peace, all who trust in you, all whose thoughts are fixed on you!* (Isaiah 26:3 NLT)

> *Do not let this Book of the Law depart from your mouth; meditate on it day and night, so that you may be careful to do everything written in it. Then you will be prosperous and successful.* (Joshua 1:8).

God promises that if we focus our minds on Him we will have peace, prosperity, and success. The work required to discipline and focus your mind on God will be worth it.

What we are really after is a renewed mind. The apostle Paul challenges all of us in this, saying, *"Do not conform any longer to the pattern of this world,* but be transformed by the renewing of your mind. *Then you will be able to test and approve what God's will is—his good, pleasing and perfect will"* (Romans 12:2, emphasis mine).

Shannon Ethridge, who I mentioned earlier, challenges you to go on what she calls a "starvation diet." This diet isn't about food but rather about starving your mind of media images that can weaken your mind against sexual integrity. She challenges you to not watch the daytime or evening soaps or talk shows that make a mockery of God's plan for sex, and she challenges you to stay away from MTV and its music videos and steamy reality shows. She challenges you to not read sex-filled "romance" novels and to not read teen magazines that put impure images in your mind. Basically, do not allow any form of pornography to enter your mind. Shannon makes a thirty-day challenge to resist worldly sexual messages and see if it doesn't help you live out the Purity Code.[1] I put the same challenge before you.

Now put the words *"I can do all things through Christ who strengthens me"* (Philippians 4:13 NKJV) into your mind. With a renewed mind, what is holding you back from becoming the person of your dreams? With a renewed mind you can live the Purity Code.

Discussion Starters

1. What ways have you seen people put bad things in their minds?
2. How do you think poor choices in what people watch, listen to, or read can affect their quality of life?

3. In this chapter, there is a principle of *starving your mind* of poor choices. What does that mean in practical ways?

4. What do you see as the importance of the Bible verse that says, "Do not conform any longer to the pattern of this world, but be transformed by the renewing of your mind" (Romans 12:2)?

CHAPTER SIX

Radical Respect:
Relating to the Opposite Sex

Some of my friends would have a hard time believing that I would write about relating to the opposite sex. After all, I'm the guy who on his very first date spilled an entire plate of spaghetti down the front of his shirt. The plate landed upside down on my lap—and I was wearing white pants. I'm the guy in high school who went to pick up a date on the wrong night, arriving at her door just as she was leaving with her older and bigger boyfriend with whom I thought she had broken up. Even my wonderful wife, Cathy, fell asleep on our first date on the way to dinner. Really!

Well, I may not have hundreds of dating success stories, but I do know that love, dating, and relating to the opposite sex are important factors in living out the Purity Code. I believe that how you relate to the opposite sex and how you eventually date will determine the success of relationships and say a lot about your Christian commitment.

You may be thinking, *But I don't date yet.* That depends on what you consider dating to be. It's true, many people think a date has to be romantic and expensive. But dating actually happens any time you are relating to the opposite sex. Driving together to camp in your parents' SUV with two guys and three girls could be considered a form of dating because guys and girls are relating. Walking home from school together is a date. Sure, it's not roses and a candle-lit meal, but you are with someone of the opposite sex, and there is interaction so that is part of the dating process. I think our culture has put way too much pressure on you to have romantic dates when in reality there are lots of other kinds of dates besides the romantic rendezvous.

Radical Respect

Far too many people who call themselves Christians do not have a clue that there is a better way to relate to the opposite sex than what the world shows us. The better way is what I call *radical respect.* This means that we are called to treat the opposite sex with a special kind of respect because Christ lives within them. This may just be one of the most important lessons related to living out the Purity Code. There really is a major difference between the world's philosophy about dating and the Christian approach. The apostle Paul summed up the Christian attitude when he said: *"Do nothing out of selfish ambition or vain conceit, but in humility consider others better than yourselves. Each of you should look not only to your own interests, but also to the interests of others. Your attitude should be the same as that of Christ Jesus"* (Philippians 2:3–5). Your job is to consider another person's interest even above your own.

David and Donna are Christians. They like each other. David is not dating just Donna, a very cute girl who has a beautiful smile and a terrific personality. David is dating Jesus, who lives within Donna. David too is a very special person. He is kind, good-looking, smart, and a great soccer player. But there is more. David has Jesus Christ living inside him by the power of the Holy Spirit. This means Donna is, in a spiritual sense, dating Jesus, who lives inside David. The bottom line is, *you are to treat your date as if Jesus lives in him or her.* We are called to radically respect God's children. And if you love someone, you want the very best for that person.

This way of thinking and behaving is not just for people your age: it's also for old people like me. When I am around a woman, I can either treat her as a sister or I can treat her as a sexual object. The Purity Code says that we guard our hearts, minds, bodies, and eyes from the bad and bounce them toward the good. Deciding to follow the way of radical respect is a great discipline, and it will keep your life free of problems in the many relationships you will have with the opposite sex.

Decide *today* to relate to the opposite sex with radical respect. Start now, and as you begin a more serious approach to dating, radical respect will be a habit. Unfortunately, most of your friends will *not* choose to live by radical respect, but you will experience freedom and healthy relationships if you do choose this way of life.

You may not be dating now, but most likely you will one day. Here are a couple of other issues to think about.

Caution: Exclusive Dating May Be Hazardous to Your Love Life.

There are two kinds of dating—*exclusive* and *inclusive.* Exclusive means it's just the two of you. It's steady and it's serious. Inclusive means you are relating to many friends of the opposite sex. An inclusive date is five girls and four guys who go to the mall together. It's three guys and two girls who meet at someone's home for pizza and a DVD. Most of us have misunderstood dating. We think it always has to be one-on-one. It doesn't.

I knew a young couple we nicknamed "the clingers." Wherever they went, they clung to each other. One was rarely seen without the other. When they finally broke up, neither had any good friends because they had invested all their time and energy in each other. Here is some good advice: Even if you do have a steady boyfriend or girlfriend, don't exclude other friendships. The sign of a good relationship is that there is not a desperate need for the other person to make you happy.

Far too many people begin exclusive relationships too early. I believe that most people who began dating at an early age would tell you they regretted it. When you exclusively date at an early age, you are setting yourself up for an easier chance at breaking the Purity Code. Look at these statistics:

Age of Dating	% Who Have Sex Before High School Graduation
12 years	91%
13 years	56%
14 years	53%
15 years	40%
16 years	20%[1]

Dating Will Be a Decisive Factor in How You Carry Out Your Christian Commitment.

As I stated earlier, show me who you date and how you date, and I can tell a lot about your Christian commitment. One of the most practical ways to practice your faith is in your dating life.

When it comes to dating, I'm always asked this question: "What's your opinion about Christians dating non-Christians?" This question is more important than you might realize. First of all, let's get something straight. Christians and non-Christians have a great deal in common. As we look at the life of Jesus, He definitely spent time with nonbelievers. We should socialize with non-Christians, but I don't think Christians should be dating non-Christians on an exclusive basis (one-on-one), even if it's not serious. The Bible is clear that believers should not marry nonbelievers. *"Do not be yoked together with unbelievers"* (2 Corinthians 6:14). It doesn't say anything about dating, but in a practical sense, dating is practice for marriage.

Does this mean you shouldn't have non-Christian friends? No. Does this mean that as a Christian you won't be sexually tempted? Not necessarily. If you are a Christian and Jesus is Master of your life, then there will be a conflict of interest with someone who has a different master for their life. Remember, it's just as easy to fall in love with a nonbeliever as with a believer.

Is It Love or Infatuation?

Here's an important fact: The average person falls in love five times between the ages of thirteen and nineteen. You may have a major crush on a guy or girl; you may even think you're in love. Your parents might dismiss it as "puppy love," but puppy love is real to puppies! When I look back at my younger years, I was always falling in love with some girl. (I definitely went over my limit of five.) For me it was:

Age 12   Chris

Age 13   Jeannie

Age 14   Nancy, then Geri (Geri was a girl!)

Age 15   Marla, back to Jeannie

Age 16   Carla and Carol (at the same time!)

Age 17   Carol

Age 18   Carol

Age 19   Cathy (this one lasted!)

But there was a major difference between the love I have for Cathy and the infatuation for, let's say, Nancy. I liked Nancy, but after a few months we decided to go our separate ways. I knew I loved Cathy because we still loved each other even through the hard times.

The difference between love and infatuation is long-term versus short-term. One day, Cathy, our girls, and I were enjoying the day at the beach. I was people-watching—like usual. A group of young girls near us were very excited about the looks of a certain lifeguard. One girl loudly proclaimed, "He's such a hunk! I'm in love, I'm in love!" I asked Cathy what she thought of the lifeguard. Even she declared, "He really is very handsome." When the lifeguard slipped down from his tower and walked to the water, the one young girl said, "I want to marry this guy. I've got to meet him." I laughed about the fact that she wanted to marry him before she even met him. I wanted to say, "Excuse me, but you're not in love; you're in infatuation."

The lifeguard story may be an exaggeration for you, but far too many people make life-changing decisions in situations almost as silly. We get infatuation confused with true love. Here are some practical guidelines and questions to help you know if you are truly in love.

Do you "like" the other person? There is a difference between love and like. In too many marriages the people "love" each other but don't actually like each other. Those marriages are pretty pathetic. It's possible to love someone without liking him or her, but don't settle for that in a relationship.

Are you transparent with each other? A sign of true love is that you can share your deepest doubts and deepest dreams, disagree on the finer points, and still feel accepted.

Are you overly dependent? True love means you want the best for the other person and that you do not have an unhealthy dependence on the other person to make you happy.

Is your love (or their love) self-centered? If the question "What's in it for me?" is often asked in your relationship, then the love is selfish, and it's not true love.

Is your love for Jesus as mature as your love for each other? A love that is tied together with the love of God is the strongest kind of love. If you can't answer yes to this question, then I think your relationship is a gamble.

Does your relationship bring you happiness? I know several teens right now who are staying in a relationship even though it brings them a great deal of unhappiness. Their low self-esteem is forcing them to hang on. I have a word for them: *foolish.*

Do you practice "emotional streaking" with each other? Streaking used to be a popular fad and still happens today. Someone is naked underneath a coat, and then at a chosen time—like halftime at the football game—they take off the coat and streak naked in front of people. I know it's gross, but it happens. Likewise, many young couples "emotionally streak" by sharing too much of their souls too quickly. This forces a couple to become way too close emotionally, and eventually they will be close sexually.

Have you and your special friend committed to the Purity Code? If the answer is no, then I question the integrity of the relationship.

Love—1-Corinthians-13–style

Here is a great definition of love. Love:

- is patient
- is kind
- is not jealous
- is not conceited
- is not proud
- is not ill-mannered
- is not selfish
- is not irritable
- does not hold grudges
- is not happy with evil
- is happy with the truth

No one has perfect love but God. But this can be a great measuring tool for your love relationship. Take a look at the previous list and think of someone you love or who loves you. Now write the words "seldom," "sometimes," or "almost always" next to the words that describe your relationship. It's a good exercise to see how the relationship is really going.

Now, let me emphasize why the information in this chapter is so important to your commitment to the Purity Code: the way you begin to view the opposite sex will play a major factor in how you do with relationships. People who radically respect have few regrets about relationships, while those who don't follow the radical respect philosophy have a very difficult time living by the Purity Code.

Susan committed to the Purity Code, but she never really lived out the radical respect concept. At age twelve she made a commitment to sexual purity, which made her parents ecstatic. She was active in school, active in her church youth group, and was one of the popular kids. Most of her friendships were with people who didn't commit to the Code. Susan eventually put her mind, body, eyes, and heart at risk. A few years later she started being noticed by the guys, and she liked the attention.

At age seventeen Susan had so compromised her view of radical respect that she became sexually active with a guy who was cute and popular but really only wanted one thing: sex. She gave her body as an act of love, and he gladly accepted it as an act of lust. Susan contracted a lifelong sexually transmitted disease, and he soon dropped out of her life. Today Susan is married and takes medicine for her STD. She also speaks to young people like you and challenges you to not give your body to another outside of marriage. She knows firsthand the physical and emotional consequences. The better way is the way of radical respect.

Discussion Starters

1. In what ways does radical respect of the opposite sex take discipline and courage?
2. How can a negative dating relationship spoil even your future and more serious relationships?
3. Read 1 Corinthians 13:4–9. Why does this seem like a very good standard of relating to the opposite sex?
4. How do you think the Purity Code and the concept of radical respect go together?

CHAPTER SEVEN

The Powerful Influence of Friends

Your choice of friends plays a big part in determining the kind of person you are and will become. Let me put it to you as straightforwardly as I can: *You will become like the people you hang around with.* This means that any person will have trouble living out the Purity Code with the wrong set of friends. Someone once said, "What you tolerate in a friend, you eventually begin to imitate." This idea echoes a proverb I like: *"Walk with the wise and become wise, associate with fools and get in trouble"* (Proverbs 13:20 NLT). As this proverb relates to the Code and other aspects of life, there could not be a truer statement.

A Friendly Influence?

One of my favorite people from my days in youth ministry was a guy named Norman, who wasn't blessed in abundance with beauty, brains, or bucks. Norman did not have an easy childhood. His dad died when he was in elementary school, and though his mother was wonderful, she wasn't home much because she worked long hours to pay the bills. In no sense could Norman be called handsome. In fact, "Stormin' Norman" looked like the quintessential nerd.

What made Norman unique was that he changed friends and fads about as often as some people change clothes. I met Norman when he was entering middle school, and in the few years I was his youth minister, Norman was a:

- surfer
- punk rocker
- football team manager
- cross-country runner
- drummer in a rock band
- cowboy (and that's difficult in Newport Beach, California)
- high school band member
- drama club member
- skateboarder
- student body officer
- student leader at church
- heavy drinker
- person heavily involved with pornography

Norman moved quickly from one crowd to another. I never knew what Norman would become next. He was like a chameleon (you know, the lizard that changes hues to whatever color it happens to be near at the moment). Every time Norman changed friends he became, in essence, a different person. His new "friends" had a big influence on who he was at that moment. As you can imagine, this influence was not always positive.

Norman had a poor image of himself. One day he confided in me, "I don't really like the *real* Norman, so I'm trying to become someone I can respect. I think if I was accepted by a group of people who liked me, I'd be okay." That was a pretty deep statement for a guy like Norman. In his own way he was beginning to understand that because he didn't like himself, he was trying to be somebody else. He was also beginning to understand the important truth that whoever you spend time with has a major influence on who you become. We'll come back to Norman later in the chapter.

Choose Your Friends Wisely

Some people never really think about the strong influence friends have on their lives. Because friends do make such a difference, it's extremely important to choose your friends wisely. Let's take a friendship inventory:

1. Do your friends bring you up or pull you down?
2. What do you like and dislike about your friendships?
3. What can you do to ensure you have quality friends?
4. Do you have friends who will help you keep the Purity Code or pull you away from it?

When I was a junior in high school, I became a Christian. I realized that the crowd I had spent a great deal of time with had not been the best influence in my life. One of the wisest decisions I ever made was choosing a new group of friends that year. It was a difficult decision, but looking back, it was the *right* decision. When I attended my ten-year high school reunion, it became very clear to me just how important that decision was in my life. Ten years later, my previous friends were struggling with drugs, divorce, and failure. My newer friends were much more together—and happier.

Sure, this kind of decision is hard. If your need for love and acceptance from others is out of balance because of a low self-image, it will be even tougher. It's also true that the decisions you make today will affect you for the rest of your life. Please don't ever underestimate the influence of your friends. Choose them wisely. They just may influence you forever, and they will definitely influence your choices connected with the Purity Code.

Peer Pressure

You and I have an incredibly strong need to be loved and accepted by our friends and family. Actually, the drive to be liked is so strong that we will do almost anything to be accepted by our peers. Peer pressure will be one of the driving forces behind many of the most difficult struggles in your life.

What power causes sixteen-year-old Janet to have sex when it goes against the way she was brought up—when she knows better? What power causes Tom at age fourteen to drink a six-pack of beer with some new "friends," steal his family's car, and go for a joyride? He didn't like the taste of alcohol; he was scared to death he would get caught with the car; and he didn't even really like the guys he was drinking with. What power, what pressure causes people to do things they really don't want to do? Peer pressure.

Janet went to a new school. She wanted to be in the most popular group, but she wasn't. She didn't like her looks. When she played the comparison game, she lost. She started to hang around with a somewhat wilder group than she was used to and went to one of their parties. Janet got drunk, but she didn't realize how drunk. After a few more drinks, she was not in control of her emotions, and her decision-making process was blurred. A guy she really liked came up to her and started flirting. They started kissing, and he convinced her to go with him to a bedroom. Janet wanted to be liked by this guy so much that she allowed him to have sex with her. It was her first time. Janet got pregnant.

Tom wanted to be accepted by a group of neighborhood guys who were a few years older. He didn't want to be known as the goody-goody Christian kid. He drank too much, took his parents' car, and, with his "friends" in the car, crashed the car in downtown San Clemente, California. Fortunately, even though the car was totaled, no one was critically injured. This time they were lucky.

Make no mistake about it, peer pressure is extremely powerful. The pressure to belong and be accepted will force you to make some very tough decisions.

The apostle Paul summarized some of his deepest feelings with these words:

> *I don't understand myself at all, for I really want to do what is right, but I can't. I do what I don't want to—what I hate. I know perfectly well that what I am doing is wrong, and my bad conscience proves that I agree with these laws I am breaking. But I can't help myself, because I'm no longer doing it. It is sin inside me that is stronger than I am that makes me do these evil things. I know I am rotten through and through so far as my old sinful nature is concerned. No matter which way I turn I can't make myself do right. I want to but I can't. When I want to do good, I don't; and when I try not to do wrong, I do it anyway. Now if I am doing what I don't want to, it is plain where the trouble is: sin still has me in its evil grasp.*

It seems to be a fact of life that when I want to do what is right, I inevitably do what is wrong. I love to do God's will so far as my new nature is concerned; but there is something else deep within me, in my lower nature, that is at war with my mind and wins the fight and makes me a slave to the sin that is still within me. In my mind I want to be God's willing servant but instead I find myself still enslaved to sin.

So you see how it is: my new life tells me to do right, but the old nature that is still inside me loves to sin. Oh, what a terrible predicament I'm in! Who will free me from my slavery to this deadly lower nature? Thank God! It has been done by Jesus Christ our Lord. He has set me free. (Romans 7:15–25 TLB)

The battle against peer pressure is one you will fight the rest of your life. It will never be easy to overcome the urge to compromise your true values to be accepted by a certain group. Adults struggle with peer pressure every day. Unfortunately, it's not something you will grow out of as you get older. However, as you discover your self-esteem rooted in God's love, you can win this battle. Just because you will have to face peer pressure the rest of your life does not mean you can't have victory over it. Negative peer influence is a foe you can—and must—defeat.

Even though you may not want to hear the truth, here it is: If your closest friends experiment with drugs, the odds are very strong that you will too. If your friends are sexually promiscuous, you will eventually turn in that direction. If your closest friends view Internet porn, you will eventually view porn. We become like the people we hang around and who influence us.

A fourteen-year-old guy once asked me, "What's so important about my friends anyway?" "You tell me," I replied. After thinking about it for a while, he took out a piece of paper and wrote the following impressions:

My friends influence me on:

- what I think about myself
- what language I use
- what I think of my parents
- what I wear
- what's *in* and what's not *in*
- what I think about my teachers
- how I act
- what parties I attend
- whether studying is important
- whether or not to drink or smoke
- what is right or wrong
- whether to have team spirit
- whether I should keep going to church
- how I should spend my money
- what I want to do when I graduate from high school

When he shared the fifteenth and last item, I looked at him and said, "I think you answered your own question."

Now, let me ask you a question. Do your friends pull you up and build you up and help you live out the Purity Code, or do they hold you down and, in reality, move you in a negative direction? Only you can answer that question honestly in your heart of hearts. But don't underestimate the influence of your friends and peer pressure.

Make Positive, Healthy Friendships a Priority in Your Life

Friendship is a priceless gift from God. Few things in life are as important or as wonderful as true friendship. A good friend is a treasure beyond almost anything else in life. Is making positive, healthy friendships a priority in your life? Think for a moment of three people whom you consider to be true friends. Now take a few moments to list why you consider them true friends. I'm sure there are several reasons you think they're special.

Here's a simple but important formula. If you want true friends, then you must become a true friend. Let's consider some qualities of a true friend. A true friend is:

1. *Caring and available.* Nothing is more important than the gift of your time and genuine concern.
2. *Encouraging.* When you affirm and support your friends, you are building their self-esteem by *showing* them they are important and that you believe in them.
3. *Willing to sacrifice.* A true friend walks the extra mile and can be depended upon, even when it's inconvenient.
4. *Patient.* No one is perfect, but a true friend will endure even in times of hardship.
5. *A good listener.* Listening is the language of love.
6. *Loyal.* The Bible says, *"If you love someone you will be loyal to him no matter what the cost"* (1 Corinthians 13:7 TLB).
7. *Truthful.* Telling the truth in love sometimes means telling a friend "the way it is," even if it hurts.

Now, as you look over this list and think about your friends, how do they measure up? How do you measure up? If you need work in one or more of these areas, there's no better time to start than right now.

Christian Friends Will Usually Encourage You to Draw Closer to God

I promised you I would get back to the story of my "nerd" friend, Norman. Sometime later in Norman's high school years, he started getting much more serious about his Christian commitment and the church youth group. In the church youth ministry, he found a crowd of people who came from different groups at school, but they seemed to get along well at church. He found friends in the church who actually liked him for who he was. They didn't try to turn him into someone else. As Norman became more comfortable with his new Christian friends, he began to open up about his hurts and past mistakes. They accepted him, and he felt loved. He came to understand God's love through the unconditional love of his friends.

It took Norman a long time to believe he belonged. He was building his identity rooted in the love of Christ, though, and the acceptance of positive friendships. These friends encouraged him to live by the Purity Code. His Christian friends *showed* him that God was real, and that reality changed his life. Today, Norman is well on his way to becoming one of the most successful youth ministers in the world. Sure there is negative peer pressure, but don't underestimate positive peer influence as well. Positive friendships will help you become all that God intends for you to become. Go for it.

Discussion Starters

1. How can negative peer pressure bring a person to break their morals and values?
2. Positive peer influence is just as powerful as negative peer pressure. How can friends help you follow the Purity Code?
3. Who are your good friends who have the best influence on you? Why?
4. What can you do to become a better friend to others? Where can you find more friends who will bring you toward the Purity Code?

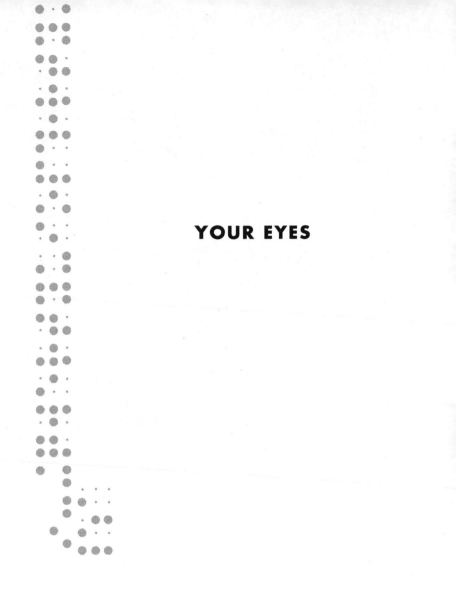

YOUR EYES

CHAPTER EIGHT

The Dangers of Pornography

At age eleven, Taylor went online to check out the baseball gloves at a sporting goods store. When he innocently typed the store's name into his search engine, he didn't find the store. Instead, he found Web site after Web site with pornographic photos of women. Taylor felt guilty and dirty. Still, he was drawn to the obscene photos, and over the next year and a half he spent time each day looking at pornographic images. His hunger for even grosser photos and stories grew, and before long he was addicted to the powerful images of pornography. His innocence was gone, and at age thirteen he was acting out some of the crude behaviors he saw on the Internet.

Taylor wasn't a bad kid. He never meant to keep looking at the porn; he just couldn't handle porn's stranglehold, and the addiction took over his life. Fortunately for Taylor, his parents finally realized what was up, and together they sought the necessary help to reprogram his mind and life. Today, Taylor is free from his pornography addiction, but he has to work at it every day. He would tell you to never start down that slippery road that brought him so much confusion, shame, and heartache. It wasn't worth it.

When it comes to the human body and sexuality, we are all curious. Frankly, curiosity is a normal and good thing. Curiosity about our bodies and sex is a part of the natural excitement that comes with the sexual awakening of puberty. That's why books like this one are written. And yet, unchecked curiosity can easily lead people into the trap of pornography. One poor decision can turn a somewhat innocent kid toward a destructive obsession that can have lifelong negative consequences.

Guys are more prone to look at porn than girls, but in today's world everyone is susceptible, and most everyone will view pornography, often accidentally stumbling upon it on the Internet.

Your Mind Takes a Picture

When you see a pornographic photo or movie, your mind takes a picture and stores it inside your brain for the rest of your life. The more pornography you see, the more photos stored in your mind— and don't think for a moment it won't affect your life.

I have been very fortunate to not view much porn, especially considering that I didn't commit to the Purity Code until I was older. Even so, there are images in my mind. This may sound silly, but in eighth grade I saw a picture of a woman with her top off in *National Geographic* magazine, which, of course, is not a porn magazine. The picture is still in my mind.

If a person does not commit early to the Purity Code, I don't know how possible it is today to refrain from viewing pornography. A few years ago I was speaking to thirty thousand students at an international youth conference in New Orleans. That night in the Superdome included an incredible time of worship, a well-known band, and literally the best laser light show I have ever seen. I challenged the students to commit to the Purity Code. Remember, the Code is much more than just not having sexual intercourse before marriage. It is committing to sexual purity, period. This includes pornography. Thousands of young people made the commitment that night. It was a pretty cool experience.

Back at my hotel room, sometime around midnight, I was channel surfing, and my eyes stopped on HBO. There it was, full-frontal nudity with amazingly gross images, right on cable TV—not even pay-per-view. My first thought was about all those high school students who were also in their hotel rooms all over the city and probably still up and watching TV. I wondered how many of them had seen the HBO program showing graphic sex.

The next day I did two workshops with four thousand students in each one. Since I was talking on healthy sexuality, it was only natural for me to ask the students how many had seen the HBO show the night before. I was floored to see half the hands go up, and I rather doubt they switched channels as quickly as I did. The power of the previous evening's commitment to purity was compromised by HBO just hours later.

As you look at your commitment to purity, you will have to see it as a battle. This battle will take self-control, discipline, accountability, and a strong faith to win.

The Porn-Addiction Progression

No one ever thinks a certain behavior they are dabbling in will cause an addiction. Porn addiction is no different. In fact, many experts say the power of pornography is very similar to crack cocaine or other drugs that hook people as quickly as the first few times. Porn addiction often starts out with a casual, almost innocent curiosity. A guy might check out a *Sports Illustrated* swimsuit issue or a Victoria's Secret catalog. Maybe a friend forwards a link to the Web site of a famous movie star scantily clothed. But the addiction escalates to wanting to see full-frontal nudity because the other stuff gets boring, and then you'll want to see sex acts, and eventually grosser and grosser things. The very nature of an addiction is that it escalates. In all, experts say there are five steps to pornography addiction.

1. Viewing Pornography.

Many boys viewed their first pornographic image in a dirty magazine or on the Internet. For many girls, the first exposure to pornographic images—either real or imagine—happened while looking at a photo of a movie star with little or no clothing, or maybe it was while reading a trashy novel or magazine like *Cosmopolitan*. For many, the first look at pornography was with a friend or at someone else's house, for example, while baby-sitting. Experts tell us that a vast majority of young people today will view porn accidentally on the Internet each month. You have more porn available and with easier accessibility than any generation before you.

Unfortunately, you will come upon porn. The purity decision you will have to make is: What will you do with it? Will you bounce your eyes? Will you linger and allow your mind to take a detailed picture? Or will you fall into the temptation of allowing your eyes, mind, and heart to take in the porn and hope it doesn't change you? What you do with what you view will determine what happens next. If you live by the Code, pornography will bother you, but you will be free to move on. If you don't live by the Code, you could easily become hooked on porn and encounter some devastating results down the road.

2. Addiction.

Perhaps the fastest-growing addiction in the world is pornography. It is enticing and exhilarating. You find yourself coming back for more. Imagine your life filled with all kinds of experiences, and now you are finding room for viewing porn on a regular basis. It begins to take over your life. Healthier experiences begin to fade away. You need the "high" of viewing porn, so you work your schedule around it. Perhaps in this phase of addiction you feel shame and guilt, and you might even try to quit, but you're hooked and you just keep coming back for more. Already you are out of control.

At this stage, you need help—quick. The longer you stay addicted to anything, the harder it is and the longer it takes to break free. I know really good kids who innocently moved into an intense addiction to pornography and were too embarrassed to get help. They prayed, they struggled, but porn's hold was too much for them. They finally had to come clean, humble themselves, and be totally honest that they needed help. Believe me, there are people who understand and want to help. Experts say that you typically can't overcome the stranglehold of an addiction by yourself.

3. Escalation.

As with most addictions, people eventually need a stronger or more intense high. For people addicted to pornography, they search for more hardcore graphic sites on the Internet. Or, while at one time they were disgusted with porn chat rooms, now they find themselves frequenting them. As your addiction escalates, so often does the frequency of the time you spend with porn. There are times when it overtakes you and becomes more important to you than anything else. A porn addict is like a drug addict desperate for a fix. The tragedy of escalation is that now the mind is filling with even more graphic and immoral pictures for your brain to store. One young woman told me that her first time with pornography was when a friend showed her an Internet site with male models and homosexual acts. She said she was "grossed out." However, she was quickly drawn back to some of those sites, and then she moved rapidly from photos to DVDs to disgusting chats even on sites like MySpace and Facebook. She told me she began to feel numb toward some of the images. Actually, at that point she was already entering the next phase.

4. Desensitization.

Desensitization is a very dangerous stage in the addiction process. The person has now seen enough graphic porn images that they are no longer excited by them. They are desperate for more thrills and willing to look at and do things that they never dreamed they would do before getting hooked. One of the strongest concerns I personally have is for the great number of guys who have already gone down this road. I have three daughters who are beautiful, and we definitely have our share of guys coming over to our house. I sometimes wonder if any of these young guys, many from Christian homes, have a secret obsession with porn.

If someone is in the desensitization stage, they are definitely viewing people as sex objects. Men objectify women as a sex object, not as a woman created in the image of God, whom we are to treat with radical respect. As discussed in chapters 1 and 2, God created our sexuality, and He sees it as "very good." God-honoring sexuality is the goal, and if someone is in the desensitization phase of pornography addiction, they are very far from having a wholesome view of sexuality. They are often more desperate to find greater thrills. The desensitization stage affects relationships with others, especially the opposite sex, and even warps our views of same-sex relationships.

5. Acting Out Sexually.

Although this might happen in an earlier stage as well, porn addicts will often make a jump from simply viewing photos and videos to fantasizing and acting out what they have seen. One guest on my radio show who was addicted to porn said, "I would have never dreamed early on when I was dabbling in porn that I would one day be driving down the street looking to hire a prostitute to try things that I thought were sick just a few months before. I lost my family. I lost my soul to porn."

The dangers of dabbling in pornography were also described to me by a very articulate sixteen-year-old who had heard me speak at a conference. He said, "I would have never invited a stripper to come into my bedroom, but yet, through porn on the Internet, I did it every night. Finally that was not enough for my cravings, so I went out and found the stripper. I was deeply disappointed and filled with shame, but I kept looking for that ultimate porn high." The young man was in for an uphill battle of reprogramming his mind and healing from his addiction. I hope you never get to this desperate place.

I walk my dog at the Dana Point Harbor most mornings and pass by people going to nearby meetings of Alcoholics Anonymous and Narcotics Anonymous. I am always so impressed by those who are in the process of working out their plans for sobriety. Complete abstinence from drugs and alcohol is the only answer for an addict.

They know they can't take a sip of alcohol or consume even a small amount of drugs. For anyone who has dabbled in pornography (and even those who have not seen it!), the answer is the same: Abstain from porn. It will only take you down a road that you do not want to travel. No short-lived, tantalizing experience is worth a lifetime of struggle.

The Internet and Porn

When I was young, the place most guys viewed pornography was in *Playboy* magazines. The images were strong, and the mind took lasting pictures. Today, however, the availability and intensity of porn for both guys and girls is so much greater because of the Internet. As I have shared, even an occasional peek at porn on the Internet can pollute your mind. Talking sexy and flirting online will also take you to places you don't want to be.

Let me tell you a story about a young woman named Lindsay. She was a good student who was active in sports and in church. Through her MySpace account, she met a guy living in another state. In their online chats, she lied and said she was nineteen, but she actually was much younger. He also said he was nineteen, though he was twenty-seven. Over time, their MySpace relationship turned to sexual conversations, and they moved from MySpace to very graphic video chats. Then came long-distance phone calls.

Lindsay thought she was in love; she had never shared her feelings so freely with a guy. She decided to come clean and tell him how young she really was. He said that was all right because he liked younger girls. He still didn't tell her he was twenty-seven, though. Finally they decided to meet. To make a long story short, she rode her bike to a nearby motel where they met in person for the first time and had sex. She loved the experience, and he flew back home.

Lindsay was still getting good grades, running cross country, and active in church. At the same time, this relationship with the young man of her dreams continued. Then one day, he let her know that he had gotten another girl pregnant and was breaking up with Lindsay. She was devastated.

Lindsay managed to keep the guy a secret from everyone, but soon her depression was so evident that her mother took her to a counselor and psychiatrist. The psychiatrist prescribed an antidepressant. Finally one night, she was curled up in a ball crying her eyes out when she told her mother the story. Her mom pulled the plug on Lindsay's computer and began a process of pressing charges against the adult who had abused her daughter.

One day Lindsay's mom and dad went to church. Lindsay said she didn't feel well. When her mom and dad came home, they found Lindsay dead. She had killed herself.

Keeping the Purity Code

I know Lindsay's story is horrible, but it shows what can happen when even good kids make disastrous decisions. She wasn't smart enough to recognize a sexual predator and understand what had happened. Few people are.

Keep to the Code, and you will never destroy your life in this manner. Here are three quick lessons for staying free of pornography.

1. Run From It.

The Bible says, *"Flee from sexual immorality"* (1 Corinthians 6:18). *Flee* means to take off running. When I was young, I was afraid of the dark. Okay, I'll admit it: there are times when dark places still give me the chills! If I was ever in a dark place, I would start sprinting toward the light. That is what you should do if you encounter pornography: Run away from it as fast as you can. In the Bible, the wife of a man Joseph worked for tried to tempt him. She took hold of his coat and said, "Come to bed with me." Do you know what he did? He ran away, and all she got was his coat.

Make a decision that you will keep your eyes pure from porn. When you accidentally encounter porn on the Internet, delete it or move on without staring and tell a parent about it. When someone shows you a DVD with sexual images, leave the room. When you are channel surfing and a sensual image appears, turn the channel and don't look back. There is no trashy book that will bring you health. Also, do not share any personal information on the Internet and do not chat with people you don't know. If you were in a dark vacant alley, there is no way you would talk with a stranger, let alone flirt with them. That is what people are doing on the Internet every day. Make the decision to never use the Internet in a sexual manner. It just might be your life that you save.

I tell parents they are in the protection business—that they should do what they can to keep unhealthy images away from their kids. You too can have an active part in this process, though. Talk to your parents about getting software that will block bad Web sites. Figure out a place everyone in the family can see the computer and use it. Come up with family agreements about things like what types of TV shows and movies are okay and how the Internet will be used. Creating boundaries in your mind and taking actions that keep you free from porn will help you live the Code.

2. Get Help Quickly.

If you have encountered too much pornography, get help now. Don't wait. I know you might be feeling some shame and guilt, but if you had a sickness and might possibly die, you'd probably go to the doctor and get the help you needed to get well. The same is necessary for pornography. Porn kills the soul. Without help, you may never know the freedom of a beautiful relationship in marriage. Your future kids may not have a role model of healthy intimacy.

There are people in your area who can help you through your problems and possible addiction. Believe me, they have heard worse stories than yours, and they are there to help. Don't postpone a decision to get help because of pride. You will need to get help from someone you can sit and talk with to give you the right advice to get past any problems from porn.[1]

3. Seek Accountability.

When anyone talks to me about their problem with pornography, the first questions I ask are, "Do you have at least one accountability partner? Do you have someone you can talk with freely and confess to if you need?" If they answer yes, I encourage them to talk to that person; if they answer no, I tell them I am not sure they can battle any problem with pornography without accountability. I know it can be shameful, but there is power in accountability. I meet with four men every Tuesday morning and with another friend every few months, and we all practice confession and accountability. I find I am a better husband and father because of these accountability relationships. There are times I choose a healthier lifestyle just because I know I would have to report otherwise to my friends.

So no matter what your age, it is a very good idea to find people whom you absolutely trust, whom you can confess to, and with whom you can share any problem you have. You want this person (or people) to be totally trustworthy. They should be the same sex as you, and they should be people who will pray for you, support you, and help you live by the Code. That's what sexual integrity is all about.

Discussion Starters

1. List the ways people see pornography in today's world.
2. Why do you think people say that there are extreme dangers in spending time with pornography?
3. This chapter talked about a porn addiction progressing from viewing porn to actually acting out sexually. How do you think a porn addiction can change the way we look at the opposite sex or even healthy sexuality?
4. How can a commitment to the Purity Code help in a commitment to "turn your eyes from worthless things"?

CHAPTER NINE

Flirting, Modesty, and
How Far Is Too Far?

While writing this chapter, my family went to a wonderful resort in Ixtapa, Mexico. As a natural-born people-watcher, hanging out at the beach while writing about purity is, well, interesting. Let's just say this week I have seen it all.

One young teenage girl was walking in the crowded market wearing a shirt that simply read FLIRT. The top had to be two sizes too small, and the FLIRT drew attention to her chest, which was rather developed for her age. As I watched the scene, it was obvious that men, young and old, were staring at the girl's top. It was actually gross and made me feel a bit uncomfortable that even older guys were drawn to her. When she turned around, I saw that the same word was printed across her very short shorts. I guess she chose her clothes that day according to a theme! Now, here is the deal: Whether or not she was aware of all the lustful stares being sent her way, the fact remains that what we wear and how we act plays an important part of living out the Purity Code.

Of course, it's not just the clothes we wear at the beach or lake. We had a Fellowship of Christian Athletes meeting at our house. Three beautiful female volleyball players were sitting at the meeting with about four inches of BC showing. ("BC" stands for butt crack in our family.) Every guy at the Christian meeting took a double take. I don't believe the girls were doing this on purpose, but I don't think it entered their minds that the guys were trying to see as much flesh as possible.

This chapter is not just for girls. Sure, guys tend to look at skin and body parts more than girls, but guys can be just as responsible with flirting, modesty, and creating healthy boundaries as girls can be.

Shannon Ethridge told me in an interview for my radio program that when it comes to developing personal, healthy boundaries, we have to guard our bodies against the "weak links of compromising clothes, compromising company, and compromising actions." I could not agree more. One of the battles most teens end up having with their parents is over those three issues. I know my wife and I did with all three of our daughters. So, let's take a look at these challenging issues through the grid of the Purity Code.

Compromising Clothes

When I was in sixth grade, I bought a pair of blue tennis shoes with my own money. My dad was not okay with blue tennis shoes! He had only seen white and black, and if that was good enough for him, it was good enough for me. Believe it or not, tennis shoes in different colors had just become popular. (Okay, I'm an old guy.) Years later when I reminded my dad of that story, he'd laugh and deny it.

He had become a cool grandpa who wore skater shoes of all different colors! Dad was wrong back then. Blue tennis shoes were probably not a battle worth fighting for. However, today some clothing issues are a problem. Let me speak to you for a moment like a dad.

Girls: Guys look at skin. So if you are showing skin, guys are checking you out. My daughter Rebecca is beautiful. When she was in eighth grade, she went to church one day in clothes that were a bit too revealing. She didn't look trashy, but I decided to use it as a learning lesson. "Rebecca," I said, "I hope you enjoy being out in this outfit today because it is the last time you will wear it. I can see your underwear and bra. Guys look at stuff like that." I hoped her response would be, "Thanks for your input, Dad. I really appreciate it, and I'll change clothes immediately. You're the best!" Instead, my comment was returned with something more like a disgusted look and the words, "Dad, you are so old-fashioned. Guys don't notice. Plus, *everybody* wears outfits like this!"

Later that day, Rebecca and I went out for frozen yogurt and then shopped for a more appropriate outfit. Basically, I bought the old outfit from her and bought her a new one too. I realized this lesson was going to cost me, but I figured it was worth it. During the time we were hanging out and eating yogurt, I mentioned to her that *men tend to have a weakness for women's bodies.* She again told me I was gross and she didn't agree. I challenged her to ask her guy friends. Later I found out they all agreed with me!

I wasn't asking Rebecca to dress like a grandma, and I'm not suggesting you should either. I just want girls and guys to rethink what they have in their closet and dresser drawers and choose clothes that are stylish and also honor the Purity Code. I am absolutely convinced that you can wear really cool, in-style clothing and do not have to compromise your commitment to purity.

If you show too much skin or wear tight clothes, you have to ask the question, "Am I teasing guys?" One person I know says that we should consider who our fashion role models are and if they help us honor God with the Purity Code. If your fashion role models come from any of the latest teen fashion and gossip magazines, you probably will have a problem answering that question positively.

My friend Hayley DiMarco made a really blunt but good point about teasing with your clothes or actions with something she wrote called the "Gross Guy Note."

> If you still don't buy the whole teasing thing, then think about it like this. It's really gross, but it has to be said: when you tease (or you just dress like one), every guy who sees you has a chance to make a movie of you in his mind—a movie rated anything he wants, like PG-13, R, or even XX. When you show off too much of yourself and creepy guys see you, I guarantee that they are taking you home with them in their minds. And I don't know about you, but I don't want to be the star in some guy's nightly fantasy. Eww![1]

Compromising Company

We have already discussed in chapter 7 how friendships play a major role in who you are and who you will become. If you hang out with kids who flirt and talk about sex a lot, then you are entering the slippery slope of sexual compromise before you even get started.

When I was in junior high, I hung out with a guy who would describe in detail what he would like to do with girls. He had a dirty joke for every occasion. I was sometimes grossed out by what he said, but I have to admit my curiosity would get the best of me and I would always come back for more. Eventually, not knowing about the Purity Code, I began to compromise some of my behavior to fit in with him. I'm grateful that he moved away and I switched friends, or I might have found myself in trouble.

The Bible has a great insight: *"Bad company corrupts good character."*[2] The point is clear: If your friends dress a certain way, you will probably end up dressing that way too. If your friends act a certain way, you will probably follow. I even know one girl who had to quit watching romantic chick flicks and reading romance novels and sexually oriented magazines like *Cosmopolitan*. She told me all her friends were into that kind of stuff, and she almost felt like she was addicted. Moving away from impure things and maybe even certain friendships may be the best decision she could make for her purity.

Compromising Actions

I am not alone in warning students about watching porn on the Internet and other obvious actions that will compromise a person's purity. However, as a dad, I want to mention a few other things that can get in the way of the Code.

Guys flirt with their hands, emotions, and words. When guys have their hands all over a girl, even if it looks like they are teasing, it is flirting. When guys talk about sexual things in a teasing way, they are flirting. If a guy is playing with a girl's emotions, he is most likely flirting. I flirt with my wife and she flirts with me. That's natural and good. But when people flirt for the wrong reasons, it is very possible that it can lead to compromising and even sometimes dangerous situations. One girl told me about the time she innocently started rubbing the back of a guy she had met at camp. He then asked if he could return the favor, but as she said, it pretty quickly turned into "more than a back rub, with his hands moving to some very private parts." She said she had no idea what to say or do, so she just let him have his way with his hands. She should have said "Stop!" but she also should not have put herself in that situation.

It is time to add things to the "don't go there" list of compromising actions, some not-so-obvious things like the tickle fight, massage, and even some forms of hugs. I'm not a prude; I just know that playful touching is not as innocent as some would think. For example, when guys go to their first middle school dance, many of them are trying to decide whom to slow dance with, hoping they get a chance to press against her breasts. Sorry if this offends you, but it's true.

Part of growing up is relating to the opposite sex. Don't get me wrong; I love the fact that girls and guys can have fun together. It's just that certain actions will and won't help all of us follow the Purity Code. The Bible says that we are not to let our brother or sister stumble. So, what may be no big deal to you may be a big deal to someone else.

My friend Jill told me that when she was dating her (now) husband, they would periodically take naps next to each other. I said, "I bet that tempted John." She laughed at me and said, "Absolutely not." I said, "Ask your husband." The next day she came back to me and sheepishly said, "You were right. John told me it was very tempting and difficult for him." So, this is why your parents will probably put limits on your alone time with the opposite sex, lying beside each other, and keeping the door open in all rooms you are in together. They will probably challenge you to not go to the wrong place at the wrong time with the opposite sex. They will undoubtedly challenge you to not talk about sex with your boyfriend or girlfriend. Again, it's not because sex is bad or wrong, but the temptations are strong at any age.

Creating Safe Boundaries

As you grow and develop through the teen years and beyond, one of the key secrets to living by the Purity Code is creating safe and healthy boundaries with your life. Personally, I use what I call the Ephesians 5:3 test, which says, *"But among you there must not be even a hint of sexual immorality, or of any kind of impurity, or of greed, because these are improper for God's holy people."* Basically this test keeps me honest about my motives and helps me be intentional about creating safe boundaries.

Here are four very important boundaries or limits to keep working on and following in order to live by the Purity Code.

1. Keep Your Eyes Free of Sexual Sights (sites).

The Bible says your eyes are the *"lamp of your body."*[3] As we have talked about before, it is impossible to avoid negative sexuality, but the key is what you do when you view it: bounce your eyes, turn your head, turn off the computer, change the channel, or excuse yourself from the movie. This takes major discipline. But it first requires a commitment that turns into action. Nobody said it would be easy, but it is still the right thing to do.

Paul gave Timothy some great advice, *"Train yourself to be godly."* (I mentioned this Scripture in chapter 5.) In today's sex-absorbed world, it will take discipline and God's strength to keep you free from the garbage that will come your way. Don't underestimate the power of lust: it often starts with our eyes and moves to our minds; then it reaches into our hearts and is sometimes acted out with our bodies. All four of those areas of your life are tied to your soul and a commitment to the Code.

2. Set Standards Now.

If you want to live with sexual integrity and purity, you will have to "pre-think" your sex limits. When I spoke to my youth group about sex, the question students asked most often was, "How far is too far?" Actually, that is the wrong question. It's not how far can you go, but how far *should* you go?

Now is the best time to write out and commit to a plan for sexual purity. Don't wait until you are dating. That is sometimes too late. Create the plan before you ever have a relationship. Talk about the plan with your parents if possible, or someone else you trust from your church or school. Then, when you have the plan in place, you can ask them to help you keep focused with your plan for purity.

3. Commit to an Alcohol- and Drug-Free Lifestyle.

You may be wondering why I would suggest this lifestyle boundary in a book on sexual purity. Let me tell you about Julia. At age fifteen she had never had a drink of alcohol. Her friends and priorities had been slipping since middle school, but she had stayed fairly strong with her commitment to not drink. Now, though, she was running with a bit rowdier crowd. Most of them did drink, and she had been at a few parties where there was drinking, but she still didn't consume. Enter Robert. Robert was seventeen, a star football player, and in Julia's words, "a hunk." She met him at a party, and he paid a great deal of attention to her. Robert had a beer in his hand, and she could tell it wasn't the only beer he had drunk that night. He offered her a drink. She didn't want to look uncool, so she drank it. No big deal, she thought. He handed her another. She wasn't sure how many beers she drank, but when we later talked, it wasn't the beer she worried about. She was worried that she had gone all the way with Robert. She apparently had passed out, and when she woke up, her underwear was not where it should have been. She was so scared. Fortunately for Julia, she wasn't pregnant, but how sad to think that her first sexual experience happened while she was passed out with a guy who totally took advantage of her naiveté.

Here is the deal. When you drink or take drugs, you lose control of your ability to make good decisions. Far too many young people lose their inhibitions and end up breaking the Purity Code because they literally were not in their right mind. Not all stories are as bad as Julia's, but you might be surprised by how many students say they broke the Code because of being drunk or high. A recent study reported that "as many as 70% of college students admit to having engaged in sexual activity, primarily as a result of being under the influence of alcohol, or to having sex they wouldn't have had if they had been sober." [4] Now *that* is a remarkable finding about the power of being under the influence of a mind-altering drug like alcohol. Besides it being against the law for you to drink, it can take you to a place you really don't want to go.

4. Don't Flirt With "Technical Virginity."

This is the section I wish I didn't have to write. If you were older, I would be even more direct and graphic. There is a growing trend with preteens and young teens to engage in oral sex. When my youngest daughter was ten, this subject was in the news a lot because a former president had engaged in oral sex with a White House intern. He point-blank said that oral sex is not sex. He may have been a brilliant person, but he was sure wrong on this point. My daughter heard all the talk on the news and innocently asked, "Daddy, what is oral sex?"

In case you haven't figured it out yet, I feel pretty comfortable talking about this subject. (You or your parents may think I am too comfortable!) But having my ten-year-old daughter ask me that question was almost too much! In the most discreet way I could, I explained that oral sex was when someone puts their mouth on another person's genitals. Of course, she thought it was gross. However, the number of even late elementary and middle schoolers now participating in oral sex is frightening. A very large percentage of girls who do this still consider themselves virgins—"technical" virgins. Another term for some of these same kids is "friends with benefits." Believe me, having a sexual relationship with a "friend" is anything but uncomplicated or casual.

Pam Stenzel is one of the finest speakers in the country today to students on sexuality. If you think I'm blunt, you should listen to her. Here is what Pam says about the issue of being a technical virgin: "The medical line that defines sex is this: Any genital contact at all, hand to genital, mouth to genital, or genital to genital, is sex." She adds, "If you have had genital contact at all, you have had sex."[5]

Too many young people today think they are following the Purity Code if they do everything but have intercourse. I disagree. Often "everything but" leads to "everything gone." Not only do some people say that oral sex is actually more intimate than genital to genital sex, but oral sex often leads to intercourse.

The time to make decisions about all this is now. Choose to live by the Code fully and be willing to go against the grain of the culture. I have a T-shirt that reads No Regrets. Make that a theme for your life as well.

Discussion Starters

1. Was there anything in this chapter that you disagreed with or thought was just too conservative?
2. Why do you think I chose the word *compromise* when I talked about clothing, company (friendships), and actions?
3. How can you personally still look in style but not violate certain standards of purity? Why can it be hard both to be in style and live with purity?
4. Creating safe boundaries was a theme in this chapter. What are some safe boundaries you could create to help you live by the Code?

YOUR HEART

CHAPTER TEN

Grace and Forgiveness

A few years ago, I heard a story about a man dressed in a very nice business suit who caused quite an uproar in downtown Chicago. One bright, busy morning, with thousands of people going about their business on Michigan Avenue, this nicely dressed gentleman stood on a street corner, pointed his finger at another man, and shouted, "Guilty!" People nearby assumed the two men knew each other. They didn't. The first man then walked farther along, pointed at another stranger, and again screamed at the top of his voice, "Guilty!"

For more than three hours, this distinguished-looking man walked Michigan Avenue. He would stop, turn, point, and shout, "Guilty!" At first people thought he was crazy. Literally hundreds of people began following him, watching his routine. Some thought maybe he had some spiritual insight because everyone he pointed to knew they were guilty in their heart of hearts. "How did he know?" they began to ask. Was he a prophet? Finally, just as quickly as he had appeared, he left and was never heard from again.

Why all the commotion about this guy? Possibly because at the core of every human being there is a sense of guilt. We all feel we've missed the mark—and we're right. The Bible puts the bad news this way: *"For all have sinned and fall short of the glory of God"* (Romans 3:23). The Bible also tells us the price of sin is death, or spiritual separation from God. The verb "to sin" means literally to miss the mark. If you think of a target and what happens when the arrow misses the bull's-eye, then you understand what it means to miss the mark. God is perfect; we are not. Because we are not perfect, we miss the mark set by God's righteousness. That's why we feel guilty, and that's bad news.

The way I best remember the term "to miss the mark" is one of my more embarrassing stories. In college Cathy and I had become what our friends called an "item." We were now boyfriend and girlfriend. I had not yet kissed her, but every night for months I had practiced kissing her on my pillow. (I don't believe I'm actually telling this story!) Each night I would close my eyes, tilt my head, and imagine kissing Cathy on the lips. The night came when I had this special feeling that I would actually get to kiss the real thing instead of the pillow. We had gone to a Christmas party, and when I walked her to her dorm room, somehow I knew this was the moment I had been waiting for. I closed my eyes, tilted my head, and, the next thing I knew, I felt something strange on my lips. I opened my eyes to see that I had missed her lips and kissed her right nostril! I drove home that night screaming in my car, "I missed her lips! I missed her lips!"

Okay, I think you get the picture on missing the mark. Now for the good news. There is hope for those who aren't perfect! We do not need to remain guilty of missing the mark. In Christ, we can be set free from our sin. That's great news! Let me tell you from the beginning: When you commit to the Purity Code, there will be times you will miss the mark. The temptations are strong and life is complicated. Hopefully you won't fall prey to some of the most difficult temptations we have already talked about in this book, but you will often need to be reminded that God's love knows no limits, and we can experience grace and forgiveness. The interesting thing is that the concept of grace and forgiveness does not lead us away from wanting to do what is right, but it leads us toward wanting to please God with purity. Let me explain.

God's ways are different from ours. Many people who have good intentions when it comes to the Purity Code have some real misconceptions when it comes to their view of God. Some think God is a God of works. They think we must *earn* His love the way we earn grades in school. They are wrong. Our God is the God of grace. Grace means unmerited favor. In other words, you don't have to do anything to receive His love. The New Testament puts it this way: *"For it is by grace you have been saved, through faith—and this not from yourselves, it is the gift of God—not by works, so that no one can boast"* (Ephesians 2:8–9).

Others think God is slow to forgive. Maybe they live in a family where people hold grudges. But God's forgiveness is ours for the asking. Humans hold grudges and remember wrong deeds. God actually forgets confessed sin. We are the ones who keep bringing up the past. God gives us a clean slate. I like what a pastor said about forgiveness: "You have no right to dredge up anything that God has forgiven and forgotten. He has put it behind His back." God's ways are different from ours, and if we are ever going to truly live by the Code, we must learn His ways.

God Loves You Unconditionally

You are loved not for what you do, but for who you are. If you're anything like me, you believe, you doubt, you get discouraged, you fight with those you love, you compromise your actions to be accepted, you justify your shortcomings, you go against God's best for you, and yet *God loves you for who you are.*

To be set free, you must come to believe that God loves you as you are and not as you should be. When one of my precious daughters skinned her knee as a youngster, I didn't yell, "You stupid kid! You are the dumbest child in all of California." I picked her up and reassured her that everyone stumbles and falls as they learn to walk—and run.

The unconditional love of God is expressed beautifully in this story about a woman caught in sexual sin:

> *Jesus went to the Mount of Olives. At dawn he appeared again in the temple courts, where all the people gathered around Him, and he sat down to teach them. The teachers of the law and the Pharisees brought in a woman caught in adultery. They made her stand before the group and said to Jesus, "Teacher, this woman was caught in the act of adultery. In the Law Moses commanded us to stone such women. Now what do you say?" They were using this question as a trap, in order to have a basis for accusing Him.*
>
> *But Jesus bent down and started to write on the ground with his finger. When they kept on questioning Him, he straightened up and said to them, "If any one of you is without sin, let him be the first to throw a stone at her." Again he stooped down and wrote on the ground.*
>
> *At this, those who heard began to go away one at a time, the older ones first, until only Jesus was left, with the woman still standing there.*

Jesus straightened up and asked her, "Woman, where are they? Has no one condemned you?"

"No one, sir," she said.

"Then neither do I condemn you," Jesus declared. "Go now and leave your life of sin." (John 8:1–11)

What a story! Picture for a moment all those men holding rocks in their hands, ready to stone this woman to death for being caught in the very act of committing adultery. (I've always wondered what happened to the man in this story who also committed adultery.) What did they think Jesus would say? After all, the Law of Moses gave them the right to kill her. Jesus simply looked in their condescending eyes and said, "If any one of you is without sin, let him be the first to throw a stone at her." Knowing full well that they too had missed the mark of God's righteousness, they all turned around and left. Christ's point was made loud and clear.

In this story, we hear a warm conversation between a woman who had missed the mark and the Lord who had every right to kill her. Showing deep compassion and unconditional love, He asked her where her accusers were. She probably looked around just to make sure, and said, "No one is left, sir."

Jesus then showed the world the true character of God's love when He said, "Then neither do I condemn you." Did Jesus say her sin was okay? Not at all. In fact, He told her to leave her life of sin. But the words "neither do I condemn you" are the same words He says to Christians even now. He loves you completely and unconditionally.

Far too many people make a commitment to sexual purity and then blow it with their body, eyes, mind, or heart. They are so defeated that they try to break their relationship with God. But God never quits loving us. His love remains strong. It is our love that wavers, not His.

Notice that Jesus didn't break a relationship with that woman who was caught in the act of adultery. Instead, He told her to leave her life of sin because He knew what would be best for her. That illustration is an incredible one of God's unconditional love and grace.

God's Love Is Sacrificial

Here is a fact that must be forever placed in our minds: *"God demonstrates his own love for us in this: while we were still sinners, Christ died for us"* (Romans 5:8). If you ever doubt God's love for you, then look to the cross. I am convinced that if you were the only person ever born into this world, Christ still would have sacrificed His life for you so that you could have a relationship with God.

Sometimes I need to be reminded of the actual physical pain and humiliation Christ went through for people who really don't take Him all that seriously. His sacrifice on the cross is the reason we can have a positive self-worth and live by the Purity Code. Because we all have missed the mark, none of us can honestly look at ourselves and feel *really* good. Purity, however, is available to us because it is rooted in the sacrificial love of God.

I like most people. However, I didn't like Clark (not his real name). Some years ago six-year-old Clark lived in our neighborhood. He declared he wanted to marry our daughter Christy, who was also six at the time. Clark had a horrible mouth and was a bad influence on our girls. One summer day Clark was out in the middle of the street as I was driving home from work. I honked my horn to get him to move out of the road, and he flipped me the international sign of displeasure! I think you get the picture.

Now, let me tell you about a dream I had in which Clark and my three girls—Christy, Rebecca, and Heidi—are playing with a beach ball in our front yard. Clark is being his typical ornery self. I'm watching from the front porch. The ball goes out into the street, and my girls go after the ball. At the same time, I see a huge truck racing around the corner. There is no way the truck can stop in time. Without a moment's hesitation I rush to the street. I smell the burning rubber of tires skidding. I push the girls aside, and just before I get crushed, I wake up. Whew!

I know that I would sacrifice my life for my children. After all, I love them and have a principle role in molding the women they will become. Now, back to my dream. Again, I watch Clark and the girls play with the beach ball. This time when the ball goes into the street and the truck races around the corner, Clark starts to run toward the ball. He is going to get crushed, and I . . . stop. I hesitate, and then I wake up. (Clark is still hanging around, so I'm sure it's just a dream.) I'm not sure I would have given my life for Clark.

God showed us how much He loved us even while we turned our backs on Him. Jesus suffered and died on the cross. Now *that's* what I call sacrificial love.

In Christ You Are Forgiven

God makes a big deal out of forgiveness. Often, forgiveness is not our style. But it is *always* His style. The concept of forgiveness goes back to the idea that God's ways are different from our ways. *God's forgiveness is forever.* Let me remind you what His Word says: *"If we confess our sins, he is faithful and just and will forgive us our sins and purify us from all unrighteousness"* (1 John 1:9). Confessed sin is forever removed from God's remembrance. Look how God describes himself to Israel in the Old Testament: *"I, even I, am he who blots out*

129

your transgressions, for my own sake, and remembers your sins no more" (Isaiah 43:25). Again we see that God not only chooses to forgive your confessed sins, but He also promises not to remind you of them.

I have a friend who is a psychiatrist. He tells me that we could empty many of the psychiatric facilities if people inside them could only understand the freedom of forgiveness. You cannot be free to be all God desires you to be without living as a forgiven person. If you are a Christian and have confessed your sin to Him, you are forgiven. Your sins are forgotten, and that's final.

Because you are forgiven, you are free to be a new creation in Christ. *"Therefore, if anyone is in Christ, he is a new creation; the old has gone, the new has come!"* (2 Corinthians 5:17). You may not feel new. At times you may not even act like a new creation. Because of Christ's sacrifice on the cross, however, you are forgiven, you are free, you are new. Go and live like it!

Let me tell you one of my favorite stories—a story that illustrates for me what it means to become a new creation of God. In the musical *Man of La Mancha,* we meet Don Quixote sitting in a pub in Spain with his faithful servant, Sancho Panza. Don Quixote is a lonely Spanish gentleman who believes he is a knight in the king's service. He isn't really a knight, but no one can tell him differently.

His waitress in the pub is Aldonza, a waitress by day and a prostitute who sells herself for sex by night. (She was definitely not living the Purity Code!) Don Quixote takes one look at her and declares, "You shall be my lady. Yes, you are my lady. You will no longer be called Aldonza, you shall be *Dulcinea.*"

She laughs scornfully and shouts, "I'm no lady!"

"No, you are my lady. You are Dulcinea," says the delusional Don Quixote.

You see, every knight needed a proper, respectable lady to inspire him in battle and to whom he would dedicate his victories. Don Quixote believed this prostitute, Aldonza, to be his lady. Later in the play, some men take advantage of Aldonza. She is raped, the ultimate indignity. After the men have abused her, she comes back into the pub, sobbing. She is hysterical. Her blouse and skirt are torn.

Don Quixote cries out, "What is wrong, my lady?"

She can't handle him any longer and screams at the top of her lungs, "Don't call me a lady! I was born in a ditch by a mother who left me there naked and cold and too hungry to cry. I never blamed her. I'm sure she left hoping that I'd have the good sense to die! I'm only Aldonza. I am nothing at all!" And she rushes into the night devastated.

Don Quixote calls after her, "But you are my lady, Dulcinea."

In the final scene we see Don Quixote lying in bed, sick and confused with fever. His faithful servant, Sancho Panza, is by his side. His family, who never believed him to be a knight, is in the room. They are simply waiting for him to die. Don Quixote is moving in and out of consciousness. There is a knock at the door, and in enters a Spanish woman in a beautiful, long gown, her head held high, her walk proud and dignified.

She goes to Don Quixote, gets on her knees, and puts her hands on his shoulder. She says, "Do you remember me?"

The family tells her he is dying, that he has lost his mind. She shakes Don Quixote and says, "You must remember me. I am Dulcinea. You gave me that name."

For a moment, Don Quixote regains his senses and stares at her. He says, "My Dulcinea, I knew you would come." He smiles and then he dies. Don Quixote believed in Aldonza, and she became what he believed her to be.

God believes in you. Because of the forgiving power of Christ, you are a new creation *no matter what you've done or who you are.* God's love transforms you into a new creation.

He believes in you.

He loves you.

You are His child.

And because of His grace and forgiveness, you can live by the Code!

Discussion Starters

1. Why do you think there is a chapter on grace and forgiveness in a book about purity?
2. Why do you think there is so much emphasis on God's unconditional love in this chapter?
3. How can grace and forgiveness actually keep a person from making poor choices?
4. Why would it be important to ask God to help you be a person of purity?

CHAPTER ELEVEN

Handling Your Emotions

I live in a home with all girls! I grew up in a home with only brothers. Believe me, there is a difference between guys and girls. I tell people that the secret to being a dad of all girls, with all the hormones and drama in the house, is to wake up and start every day by saying, "I'm sorry. I'm sorry. I'm sorry." Guys can have intense emotions too, but they often handle them differently than girls.

I recently asked a small group of middle school students to rank the most difficult emotions from this list that they face:

Worry	Moodiness
Stress	Loneliness
Fear	Depression
Anxiety	Anger
Guilt	Passion

A very sharp young woman raised her hand and said, "You just listed my autobiography." We all laughed, but the more we talked the more we realized that, for many people, the teenage years are filled with intense emotions that can often seem out of control. Uncontrolled emotions can affect your thinking and lead to an improper self-image. When that happens, you tend to violate your values, including the Purity Code.

There's lots of talk about our fast-paced, pressure-filled world. While you're making the transition from the carefree days of child hood to the breakneck pace of young adulthood, you will be dealing with the normal "growing pains" of adolescence—social stress, body stress, school stress, parent stress, sexual stress, peer-pressure stress, religion stress, and all the rest. It's easy to snap under all that pressure.

Pressure comes from every direction. I don't remember where I came across this list of what teenagers worry about, but I like it. Teenagers just like you worry that:

- in a long kiss, you'll have to breathe through your nose and your nose will be stopped up
- your breath smells
- you have B.O.
- if you're a girl, you won't have breasts
- if you're a boy, you *will* have breasts
- if you're a boy, you'll never be able to grow a mustache
- if you're a girl, you *will* have a mustache
- when you go to the bathroom, people will hear
- the lock on the bathroom door doesn't work, so someone will walk in

Yes, emotions are strange. I'm sure that during some days there are times you will feel really down and then totally happy. As you grow older, you might be consumed with anxiety over a broken relationship and, in the very next minute, feel completely at peace. You might feel guilty about a very small mistake, or your conscience may not even be stirred when you really compromise your convictions in a big way.

Your emotions play an important part in how you feel about life. Just when you think you have tamed a certain emotion, it flares up worse than ever. Is it possible to trust your feelings and emotions? Why do you act the way you do? Are you normal or a little crazy? If these are your questions, welcome to adolescence. Nobody said it would be easy!

This chapter is not meant to be an in-depth look at your emotions but rather a practical guide to help you through the tough times.

Emotional difficulties are sure to come, but some can be avoided. In chapter 4, we discussed the physical consequences of not following the Purity Code. But there are also emotional consequences. Hayley DiMarco says, "Teenage sexual activity routinely leads to emotional turmoil and psychological distress."[1] Pam Stenzel, in her wonderful book *Sex Has a Price Tag*, summarizes all the common emotions felt when the Code is broken: guilt, depression, rejection, mistrust, sadness, loneliness, fear, worry, regret, anger, withdrawal, and self-reproach.[2] In other research, students aged twelve to seventeen who were involved in unhealthy romantic relationships had much higher levels of depression than those not involved in romantic relationships. Pam Stenzel can be very blunt, but she puts it very well: "There isn't a condom in the world that will protect your heart."[3]

I have a sign on my desk that reads No Regrets. Living by the Purity Code doesn't make all the emotional drama go away, but it will help you keep from breaking when the pressures of life hit.

Jesus concluded the greatest sermon ever preached with this illustration:

> *Therefore everyone who hears these words of mine and puts them into practice is like a wise man who built his house on the rock. The rain came down, the streams rose, and the winds blew and beat against that house; yet it did not fall, because it had its foundation on the rock. But everyone who hears these words of mine and does not put them into practice is like a foolish man who built his house on sand. The rain came down, the streams rose, and the winds blew and beat against that house, and it fell with a great crash.* (Matthew 7:24–27)

This story reminds us that rain, wind, and storms come to everyone. No one is exempt from tough times. But how you *prepare* for the storms of life makes all the difference in the world. What you do with your foundation is your choice. You can build your life on the Rock—or gamble on the sand.

Five Important Principles

Here are five principles to follow to keep your life from crumbling under pressure:

- Stay healthy.
- Develop meaningful relationships.
- Avoid negativism.
- Reach out to others.
- Live one day at a time.

Stay Healthy

You can't control everything about your health; for example, many people struggle with asthma. However, there's a strong connection between health and happiness. To combat intense negative emotions, it is important to watch what you eat, keep your body in good shape, get plenty of sleep, and set aside enough time for relaxation. How are you doing in each of these areas? If just one of these is out of kilter, you can't live life to the fullest, and you will be more vulnerable to breaking the Purity Code.

When you improve your physical life, you will feel more in control of the other areas of your life as well. When I'm tired, I am grumpy. When I've driven my body to the point of exhaustion, I am more likely to experience anger, depression, and worry. God made our bodies to function together with our minds and spirits. Odds are that if you are not taking care of your body, other areas of your life are also in lousy shape.

The Bible reminds us why we need to keep our bodies healthy: *"Do you not know that your body is a temple of the Holy Spirit, who is in you, whom you have received from God? You are not your own; you were bought at a price. Therefore honor God with your body"* (1 Corinthians 6:19–20).

If you are experiencing intense negative emotions, let your parents know and get a physical checkup. You may be dealing with a medical problem. I know a young woman who was experiencing extreme moodiness and severe depression. She tried everything to pull herself out of her despair. Finally, she visited a doctor and found that she had, along with an irregular and painful menstrual cycle, a hormonal imbalance. The doctor prescribed treatment that corrected the physical problem, and the emotional problems went away also.

As I have mentioned in other parts of this book, to stay healthy you must also keep your mind and thought patterns healthy. Counseling is a positive option for anyone who is struggling with negative thoughts. When I was in graduate school and studied counseling, it was mandatory for those of us in the program to receive counseling. At first I didn't want to go. After all, I wasn't aware of any problems. However, I can honestly say that those eight sessions with a counselor were some of the most freeing times I'd ever experienced.

Your body, mind, and spirit are all connected, so don't neglect any one of them when trying to stay healthy.

Develop Meaningful Relationships

Kristi was a song leader and an outstanding swimmer, and she was very active in my church youth group. One day she called me and blurted out, "Jim, I don't have any friends. No one likes me. No one knows me."

Kristi totally threw me a curve. I assumed that because she was active she had plenty of intimate friends with whom she could share her hurts, dreams, and joys. She said, "No one ever calls me, so I sit at home when everybody else is out doing something." As we investigated this problem together, we found out that others assumed Kristi was already busy, so they didn't bother to call. We also learned that Kristi needed to initiate relationships with others. When she made the calls and planned things with others, they were sincerely excited to spend time with her.

Perhaps the smartest move Kristi made was to launch a weekly support group with three other girls from our church. It wasn't part of the church program; they just made it happen. Those four girls became the best of friends, and their weekly meetings continued throughout high school. Kristi graduated from high school happier and healthier because she took the risk and developed meaningful relationships.

This just may be one of the best decisions you can make to stick with your decision to follow the Purity Code. Most of us have too many people we can call acquaintances and not enough people we can call close friends. Spending time with positive, uplifting people makes such a difference in your life and your emotions.

Avoid Negativism

People who are negative, critical, argumentative, and self-condemning are unhappy people. Negative thinking is simply a bad habit. Did you know it can take as little as three weeks to form a lifelong habit? The good news is you can also eliminate some of your bad habits in just three weeks. It takes work, but it's worth it.

Here's what helps me: *thank therapy.* I make it a point each day to decide whether I'm going to be a person who grumbles and complains my way through life, or to be a person who is thankful and grateful. It's really up to me. The Bible says, *"No matter what happens, always be thankful, for this is God's will for you who belong to Christ Jesus"* (1 Thessalonians 5:18 TLB). The NEW INTERNATIONAL VERSION urges us to *"give thanks in all circumstances."*

Notice that Scripture does not say to be thankful *for* all situations; it says to be thankful *in* all situations. How ridiculous it seems to be thankful for a difficult problem! But when we are challenged to be thankful *in* all circumstances, it is much easier to see that even in difficult times there are reasons to be thankful.

At one time or another, everyone begins to feel sorry for themselves. At times we feel we "got the short end of the stick." Yet it is important for us to have an attitude of thankfulness. No matter who you are or what troubles have come your way, you have many reasons to be thankful. Sometimes we need to be reminded of the old Native American proverb that says, "I complained because I had no shoes, until I met a man who had no feet."

You can avoid negativism and practice thankfulness. For me, *thank therapy* means focusing on reasons why I am thankful. I tend to have tunnel vision and forget the many, many reasons I have to be grateful. Try this: When you are feeling negative, list on a piece of paper all the reasons you can think of why you are thankful. You can't help but be less critical and negative. Practice makes perfect, so perhaps it's time to put this book down and make thankfulness a habit.

Optimism really can give you strength when it comes to making the Purity Code a vital part of your life. Optimistic people often have better self-images and better emotional health. This means they have a stronger sense of saying no to the bad and yes to the good. Try to become more optimistic and find people who are this way. It can make all the difference.

Reach Out to Others

There are two kinds of people in the world: self-absorbed, "me first," "I-centered" people and those who are "others-centered." Think for a moment about the happiest people you know. They are probably the most others-centered people you know. If you want to be happy, become a person who reaches out to others.

1. Do favors for your friends and family.
2. Give compliments.

3. Be available to serve.

4. Remember that listening is the language of love.

If you are unhappy, take a serious look at just how much of your life revolves around *you*. Self-centered people will always struggle with feelings of inferiority. I heard a story of a woman who was negative, critical, sick, and deeply depressed. She had gone from one doctor to another looking for a cure. Each time the doctors would run extensive tests and find nothing physically wrong. She finally visited a very wise old physician. Instead of just checking her physically, he listened to what he called her "me focus." He sensed she needed to quit looking inward and begin to reach out.

When he finished the checkup, he handed her a prescription that read, *Do something nice for someone else for fourteen days in a row, then come back and see me.*

"That's it?" she said.

He smiled and responded, "That's it. You try this prescription, and I think you will feel 100 percent better."

Well, she did do something nice for someone else every day for two weeks. Her gifts of service weren't earth shattering. They were more along the line of baking cookies for a lonely elderly woman in her neighborhood and actually taking the time to listen to a hurting friend. For two weeks she took joy in doing special little acts of love for others. She then realized the doctor was right. She felt better than she could ever remember feeling. Maybe we can learn a lesson from this story.

Live One Day at a Time

Jesus gave us some important advice when He said, *"Do not worry about tomorrow, for tomorrow will worry about itself. Each day has enough trouble of its own"* (Matthew 6:34). In other words, live one day at a time.

Did you know . . .

- Eighty-five percent of our worries will never happen.
- Ten percent of our worries will happen whether we worry or not.
- Only 5 percent of our worries are valid.

I know a man who lived his life by this formula: If each day is lived as it comes, each task is done as it appears, then the sum of your days will be good. He died a happy and fulfilled man.

You can live your life with purpose. Stop living accidentally, letting the winds of change carry you from crisis to crisis. Stop letting circumstances rule your emotions and determine your outlook on life. You can *choose* to be happy. You can even choose happiness in the midst of pain. Abraham Lincoln once said, "Most people are about as happy as they choose to be."

It's time to quit blaming your unhappiness on others or on your circumstances. Take responsibility for your own happiness.

Life is too short to focus on the mundane rather than on the miraculous.

Life is too short to hold a grudge.

Life is too short to let a day pass without hugging a loved one.

Life is too short to put off Bible study and prayer—to stay indoors—or settle for second best in life.

Life is too short—way too short—to choose mediocrity.

If you want to prepare yourself for the emotional storms of life that come your way, you have to start small. Set specific goals that will stretch you but are attainable. Experience little successes along the way. Growth requires effort. Even if you don't *feel* like it, do it anyway. Your feelings will often follow your actions. Never, never forget that God believes in you, wants the best for you, and is willing to walk with you through your most difficult times.

Here's a prayer that has been helpful to me and to my emotional health. It's called the Serenity Prayer.

> *God grant me the serenity*
> *to accept the things I cannot change;*
> *courage to change the things I can;*
> *and wisdom to know the difference.*
> *Living one day at a time;*
> *Enjoying one moment at a time;*
> *Accepting hardships as the pathway to peace;*
> *Taking, as He did, this sinful world*
> *as it is, not as I would have it;*
> *Trusting that He will make all things right*
> *if I surrender to His Will;*
> *That I may be reasonably happy in this life*
> *and supremely happy with Him*
> *Forever in the next.*
> *Amen.*
> —Reinhold Niebuhr

Discussion Starters

1. There are a lot of emotions that you go through every day. Why do you think that is?
2. If a person's emotions are sort of out of control, how can this lead to violating their values, including breaking the Purity Code?
3. What practical things can a person do to get their emotions under control?
4. The Serenity Prayer quoted at the end of this chapter is a great prayer for emotional health. What part of the prayer helps you the most?

CHAPTER TWELVE

Developing a Healthy Self-Image

When I walked into Mrs. Chun's fourth-grade classroom on the first day of school, there was something unique about me. It wasn't something I was very proud of. In fact, this "uniqueness" caused me a great deal of trauma and embarrassment. You see, I was the only boy in the entire fourth grade at Horace Mann Elementary School in Anaheim, California, who had hair growing under his armpits. (Actually, Priscilla Shelton also had hair under her arms, but that's another story!)

Now, this growth under my arms was not exactly a bush, mind you, but it was *hair,* and that was bad enough. In fourth grade, I wasn't sure I could ever show those hairs to anyone. The first time I remember praying was during that year when I begged God, "Please never let me be 'skins' when our basketball team plays 'shirts and skins.'" Whenever I raised my hand in class, I covered my armpit with my other hand.

You may be wondering what this story about a ten-year-old,

hairy-armed boy has to do with the Purity Code. Simply this: What happened to you when you were a kid will have a large influence on how successfully you handle your adolescent years. It has to do with how you feel about who you are, whether or not you like yourself. People with poor self-images tend to struggle more often with their sexual purity.

The armpit story is just one traumatic experience from my past. If you had the time, I could tell you about many embarrassing incidents and other experiences that adversely affected the way I felt about myself during my adolescent years. We could talk about my childhood hurts, the times I succumbed to peer pressure, and the feeling of not being accepted by so-called friends. Or we could just talk about the problems I had with my physical looks. My wife sure didn't marry me for my great hair, athletic build, or movie-star looks.

Some people call this a low or improper self-image. Ever since I can remember, I have played the comparison game—comparing myself to others around me. But whenever I play the comparison game, I always lose. Wherever I look, I see people who are smarter, more coordinated, better looking, and more talented than I. But the fact is, most of these same people (and most of the people you know) suffer from a poor self-image. It is likely that low self-esteem affects the one person you know best—yourself.

Your self-esteem, or self-image, is how you think and feel about yourself. *And how you feel about yourself will affect every part of your life, including your sexuality.* How you think and feel about yourself will determine much of your outlook on life, whether joyful, miserable, adventurous, tragic, or indifferent. Your view of life will, in turn, color your relationships with friends, family, and others. How these people respond to you takes you back to the beginning of the cycle—how they treat you will have a tremendous effect on how you think and feel about yourself. I honestly believe that much of the trouble we see in the world dealing with impure sexuality stems from people having an improper self-image.

Nicki always put herself down. Even when someone tried to compliment her on her hairstyle or clothes, she refused to accept the compliment at face value. She tended to be a complainer. Deep down inside she hated herself, knowing she was becoming a very negative person. Nicki's parents kept telling her not to be so critical of herself, but she couldn't get the negative thoughts out of her head. She didn't like her looks, and she hated her clothes. She felt that if she were taller, she would be prettier. Nicki even hated her quiet personality. There were times she resented God for not making her a different person.

Nicki was caught in a vicious cycle of low self-esteem. She didn't like herself, and her negative outlook affected how others viewed her and responded to her. Because most of her "vibes" were unfavorable toward others, she didn't receive a lot of positive support. Convinced that everyone hated her, she began to feel even worse about herself. For Nicki to break the cycle, she had to learn to like herself.

Learning to like yourself is one of the keys to making your adolescent years a positive experience and sticking with your commitment to purity. You are an unrepeatable miracle. This may be hard to believe sometimes, but you are the making of a masterpiece. There is no one else quite like you in this entire world, and that makes you someone special.

Is it easy to overcome an inferiority complex? Can you learn to feel good about yourself in ten simple lessons? The answer is an emphatic *NO*. When it comes to the struggles of life, no one said it was going to be easy. But I have great news for you. You *can* establish your own identity and learn to really like yourself. One important way is by having the right mindset about what I call the "big three."

Beauty, Brains, and Bucks

Because beauty, brains, and bucks are so highly valued in our world, they tend to be major roadblocks to building a healthy self-esteem. In actuality, none of the "big three" attributes are evil or sinful, but when placed on an unreachable pedestal, they can be devastating to your self-image.

Beauty

I'm not going to tell you to quit brushing your teeth or using deodorant! I think you should do everything you can to look attractive. However, the pressure we all are under to pursue physical perfection is frightening, especially when you consider that about 80 percent of the teenagers in our society don't like the way they look! The media has set unreasonable standards for physical appearance, making them unattainable for the vast majority of us. Yet millions of people strive to look like the latest rock stars, movie idols, and sex symbols. Now hear this: *God does not place prime importance on physical appearance or strength.* Our society does. Our world is hung up on beauty and ability. You think I'm exaggerating? Who gets more attention in life—the pretty baby or the ugly one? Who gets more dates in high school—the beauty queen or the homely girl? Who was the student body president at your local high school this year? The odds are, he or she was a better-than-average-looking person.

For most of us, the inability to accept our physical appearance is devastating to our self-esteem. The problems with our physical appearance start very young. In my seventh-grade yearbook, Eddie Hovdy wrote these words to me:

> God created rivers
> God created lakes
> God created you, Jim.
> Everyone makes mistakes.

I don't remember anything else about my seventh-grade yearbook, but those words are etched in my memory forever. To this day, I still remember reading that poem and putting my yearbook down, trying to figure out why Eddie didn't like me. I thought about all the physical characteristics I didn't like about myself. Eddie probably didn't like me because of the gap between my front teeth, my hairy legs, or my eyebrows. Besides, I was much shorter than Eddie. For days I was depressed. I hated Eddie, but I also hated myself because I didn't look as handsome as he did. Of course, Eddie probably wrote that silly poem in everyone's yearbook, but you couldn't have convinced me of this in the seventh grade.

Because physical appearance plays such an important role in our self-image, it's extremely important to understand that God does not look at your outside appearance. Very few will make it on the Mr. (or Ms.) Universe tour, so take comfort in the conversation God had with the prophet Samuel. God was talking to Samuel about a very handsome man whom God was rejecting as a candidate for the next king of Israel. God said, *"Do not consider his appearance or his height, for I have rejected him. The Lord does not look at the things man looks at. Man looks at the outward appearance, but the Lord looks at the heart"* (1 Samuel 16:7).

God simply places no importance on your physical appearance. He focuses on your inner person. God's desire is that we have real inner beauty. He wants you to recognize that He was active in your very creation (see Psalm 139:13–15) and that He is still involved in every part of your development.

Unfortunately, far too many people devote a great deal of time and attention to their outward appearance and not nearly enough to their inner beauty. You and I both know people who are stunningly beautiful on the outside and miserable on the inside. These same people sometimes sacrifice their purity for acceptance in a crowd of "pretty people" who end up as losers in life. The most attractive people I know are those who have developed an inner beauty that radiates even to the outside, making them more physically beautiful as well.

Brains

When I was growing up, there was a kid in our neighborhood named Tom, whom we nicknamed "Albert Fruitfly." We called him that because he was homely and always in the slower classes in school. I'm ashamed to say I was one of the instigators of this horrible nickname. All throughout elementary, junior high, and even into high school, we called him Albert Fruitfly. We were all amazed that Tom graduated from high school. Immediately afterward he moved from our city, and I lost track of him completely.

Out of the clear blue, nine years after high school, Tom called me to say he was coming to town on business and wanted to take me to lunch. We agreed on a time and a restaurant. I got there first. Before not too long, a good-looking business executive, who radiated confidence and intelligence, walked over to me and greeted me with a firm handshake. I would never, ever have recognized him! When we sat down, I asked Tom to tell me his story.

He said that all his life his parents had compared him with his older brother, who always received straight *A*s. Tom just assumed he was dumb and ugly, because that's what everyone told him. When he graduated from high school, he moved to another part of California. He attended a junior college and, without the negative influences, earned great grades. He started attending a Christian club on campus and eventually made a commitment to Jesus Christ. Tom learned that, in God's eyes, he wasn't dumb *or* ugly. God believed in him even when he didn't believe in himself. Tom attended university, then went on to get his MBA. He married a beautiful woman and had two great kids.

I left that lunch with two very different emotions. I was absolutely ecstatic that Tom had become such a fulfilled person. If Tom could do it, with God's help, anyone could. I also felt deep shame for taking an active part in making his early years unhappy. Please never forget that God's idea of intelligence is very different from the world's.

Bucks

A popular bumper sticker with a few variations reads, The Person With the Most Toys, Wins. What a lie. More toys, more money, or more things do not bring anything close to victory, or happiness, for that matter. In fact, they usually bring more emptiness. I'm not suggesting you should give up every nice thing you own. However, I strongly challenge you to examine whether you are building your esteem upon material stuff. If you are, then get ready for disappointment in the future. Material wealth seems to be everyone's goal these days, and many have "sold their souls" for the almighty dollar (or a certain cell phone or the latest electronic gadget or . . . you name it) lying, cheating, and stealing to get to the top financially. Contrary to popular teaching, success is not spelled M-O-N-E-Y.

A few years ago, I decided to tackle the subject of money with our youth group at church. Honestly, I had no idea what to expect. I started out with a simple discussion starter: "Let's go around the living room and share what we want to be when we grow up."

Derrick was first, saying, "I want to be rich."

"Okay," I replied, "but what do you want to do to become rich?"

He shot back, "I don't really care what I do; I just want to make a lot of money, live by the ocean, and drive a Porsche."

At first I thought Derrick was kidding, but I seemed to be the only one in our group amused by his comment. All the other students took his statement at face value. Now, this doesn't mean Derrick is a bad person, nor are any of the other students. It does mean that people who think better of themselves by worshiping money will really never have a proper self-image. I do know a lot of rich people who haven't worshiped money, but they also understand these words of Jesus about material wealth:

> *Do not store up for yourselves treasures on earth, where moth and rust destroy, and where thieves break in and steal. But store up for yourselves treasures in heaven, where moth and rust do not destroy, and where thieves do not break in and steal. For where your treasure is, there your heart will be also.* (Matthew 6:19–21)

Finances are not a side issue in our faith. Jesus spent more time talking about money than He did about love. Jesus knew money would affect our faith and commitment: *"No one can serve two masters. Either he will hate the one and love the other, or he will be devoted to the one and despise the other. You cannot serve both God and Money"* (Matthew 6:24).

You may be asking why I am spending so much time talking about beauty, brains, and bucks. The reason is simple. A wrong perspective on these issues can turn a good self-image into an improper one quickly.

Too many of your friends will start out okay and then begin to drift away just a bit. Their focus will turn to superficial things. They will make compromises to feel good about themselves and one day realize they are lost and not living by the Purity Code. You don't want this to happen to you.

The best news is that building a healthy self-image is not all left up to you. The God who created this world cares deeply about who you are and who you are becoming. The Bible says, *"For we are God's workmanship, created in Christ Jesus to do good works"* (Ephesians 2:10). This is the way I figure it: To build a healthy self-image in you, God must do His part and you must do yours. God has already done His part, so all you have to do is respond to what He has already done for you.

God's Part:

- God created you;
- He loves you;
- He accepts you;
- He forgives you;
- He values you;
- He gifted you;
- He showed you the way to purity.

Your Part:

- Put God first in your life;
- Live up to your potential.

Put God First in Your Life

Jesus said it best: *"Seek first his kingdom and his righteousness, and all these things will be given to you as well"* (Matthew 6:33). Jesus promises us that when we put God first, then our lives will be in order. Does He promise a problem-free life? No way. He does, however, offer to take care of us day by day when we make Him top priority in our lives.

People with low self-esteem have, first and foremost, a spiritual problem. Your relationship with God ultimately affects every other area of your life. When I was young and did my best to put God first, my relationships with my parents, friends, family members, and even teachers improved. Putting God first had a tremendous effect on my grades, work, health, and, very importantly, my dating relationships. When you allow God's profound love and belief in you to be placed at the center of your life, you are well on your way to living up to your potential.

Live Up to Your Potential

With God loving you and caring for you, you are free to be all He desires you to be. Basically, living up to your potential involves living a life of purity.

Let me tell you one more story about a friend I've mentioned before, Shannon Ethridge. She is one of my favorite guests on my radio program. But much more than that, she is a woman who absolutely inspires me. Shannon was raised in a home where she knew the Purity Code. She was brought up with faith in God and a desire to live a moral life. Somewhere along the way, though, a poor self-image led to compromised values. Shannon's life took a detour, and she fell into a lifestyle of relationships that were less than pure. Her sexual promiscuity and other poor choices caused her relationship with God to fade. Life seemed to be going downhill.

One morning while driving to her high school, she was looking in the rearview mirror and putting on makeup when she ran over a woman on a bicycle and killed her. Almost unbelievably, the woman's husband did not press criminal charges but instead showered Shannon with the love of Christ.

The pain and heartache from that tragic experience have been healed by God, and today Shannon is doing something so very worthwhile. She has written much about sexual integrity and her life in her books, which I highly recommend, and now with her wonderful husband, Greg, she is helping young people all over the world.

It is my prayer that you will allow your self-image to be based on God's image of you, so that you won't experience the heartbreak that comes when the Purity Code is broken. Some people can come back and do great things, but others just drift away and have many regrets.

Discussion Starters

1. Many people with a poor self-image are easily seduced sexually. Why do you think that might be the case?
2. How can a person your age not play the comparison game about others who might be smarter, better looking, more talented, or even richer? How can you become more secure with yourself?
3. How can a better relationship with God help a person's self-image?
4. What are areas of your life that you might need to work on to develop a more positive and healthy self-image?

CHAPTER THIRTEEN

Sexual Abuse

I hope you never have to experience the trauma of sexual abuse. It is one of our worst tragedies in the world. For most of the people reading this book, you probably haven't been abused, but knowing the information in this chapter can help you help others who have been abused or one day will be abused. Unfortunately, a large percentage of people do experience sexual abuse, and this is a very important chapter to read to help you understand the traumatic effects of sexual abuse and how to prevent it from happening to you.

When you were younger, your parents needed to teach you to look both ways when crossing streets and to not talk with strangers. The need to learn how to prevent sexual abuse is similar. Certain precautions don't always come naturally, but you will want to make them a part of your life.

Although I will talk more about it at the end of the chapter, make sure you understand that no one has the right to make you feel uncomfortable by a touch or word. You have the right to say no to anyone or anything that doesn't fit within the Purity Code or makes you feel uncomfortable, or even awkward. Unfortunately, the world is filled with people—some of whom we know and love—who have a warped view of their sexuality and life. If for any reason you find yourself in a difficult situation, immediately talk with your parents or someone you really trust. The effects of sexual abuse are just too devastating.

I wish you could have been with me at lunch today. I sat with one of the most outstanding men in our community. He's rich, incredibly handsome, and one of the funniest people I know. To be honest, at times I play the comparison game with him, and I always lose.

Today was different. He told me of his childhood. Tears were flowing from his eyes as he shared one of the worst sexual abuse stories I have ever heard. He has always looked so together, but on the inside, this man was falling apart in every way—all because he had been a victim of one of the cruelest crimes imaginable. His grandfather, whom he had loved and trusted, had sexually molested him year after year from ages eleven to sixteen. My friend had never told anyone, including his wife. He had buried his hurt and pain, but now, as he was coming to grips with his past, he realized his abuse was causing him agonizing torture.

This is a very serious chapter. There is nothing funny about sexual abuse. Nobody likes to talk about it, and nobody really wants to hear about it. Yet the cold, hard, frightening facts tell us that sexual abuse affects the lives of millions of people who just wish it would go away.

One out of three young women will be sexually abused by the age of eighteen.

One out of seven young men will be sexually abused by age eighteen.

These statistics actually are conservative compared to some of the latest findings, which say the problem could be far more widespread.

Sexual Abuse Is Real, and It's Everywhere

If you have been a victim of sexual abuse, these may be the first words about the subject you have read. Yet every part of your life is clouded by the fact that something very horrible has happened to you. If you have never been sexually abused, someone close to you probably knows the trauma of sexual abuse only too well.

From my counseling experience, I knew that sexual abuse was a problem. I had no idea, though, just how prevalent it was until I started speaking about the subject. Wherever I go, when the subject is brought up, people who are unquestionably devastated by their experience come to me and want to talk.

Let me introduce you to some very special people who were in my youth group when I was a youth pastor. They looked and acted like everyone else, but inside they were keeping a terrible secret that was tearing them apart. All the names and some of the situations have been changed for obvious reasons of confidentiality, but these stories are real.

Bonnie was baby-sitting at her ex-boyfriend Tom's house. She was very close to his little sister and his family, even though Tom and she had quit dating. Tom's stepfather had always been very nice to Bonnie. In fact, she often wished she had a father as special as Tom's stepfather. Tom's family was going out to dinner and to a play while Bonnie watched the youngest child. The stepfather, Ted, would be home, but he would be working in a back room.

The moment Bonnie put the little girl to bed, Ted came into the kitchen and asked Bonnie if she wanted some popcorn. Bonnie loved popcorn. She said, "Thanks. That will go good with the program I'm watching on television."

Ted made the popcorn, then sat down on the couch next to Bonnie and started watching the program with her. Bonnie complained about a sore back she had gotten from playing softball. So Tom's stepfather began to massage her back. At first he rubbed outside her sweater, but after a while he moved his hands under her sweater.

Bonnie froze. She didn't know what to do. She didn't know if this "nice" man was going to go further or was just doing her an innocent favor. Bonnie was tense and nervous. In a soft voice Tom's stepfather told her to relax; it would be better for her backache. Eventually, Ted began feeling her breasts. The phone rang. Bonnie was grateful for the distraction. Tom's stepfather—reluctantly, it seemed—got up to answer the phone. Bonnie had been sexually abused.

When Monica was nine years old, her fourteen-year-old brother molested her. It was a terrible, traumatic experience, which she revealed to no one because her brother threatened to kill her if she told. The next month, her brother raped her. For the next two and a half years, he had sexual relations with her, always vowing to kill her if she told anyone.

Monica never told a soul. Her brother was a violent person, and she feared for her life. She withdrew. She flunked most of her classes and experimented with drugs given to her by her brother. Finally her brother was arrested for armed robbery, and Monica was free of the horror of further traumatic experiences.

An acquaintance of Monica invited her to a weekend retreat at a Christian camp. There, for the first time in her life, she heard about God's unconditional love for her through Jesus Christ. She wanted to become a Christian, but her past experiences haunted her and kept her from accepting Christ. After coming home from camp, she made an appointment with a youth pastor and told her story. Monica had been sexually abused.

Steve was seven when a baby-sitter molested him.

Janice, at age nine, heard her parents fighting terribly one night. That evening, for the first time, her father slipped into her room and had sexual intercourse with her. This pattern continued for the next seven years.

Tom's favorite uncle molested him on a camping trip and confused Tom by telling him that all uncles "do this" with their favorite nephews.

Older boys in the neighborhood sexually abused Carol. When she told her parents, her mother didn't believe her. Carol's father laughed.

All these people had been sexually abused.

The stories go on and on. Just in the past few months, I have heard horror stories of a man videotaping a young girl in the shower, older males exposing themselves to innocent children, a date rape, adults sharing pornographic photos with children, and other stories I can't put into writing. Sexual abuse is real, and it's everywhere.

Good News for Victims of Abuse

Unfortunately, most people who have been sexually abused in one way or another keep their pain and experiences to themselves. They try to forget about it or simply wish it would go away. Well, it doesn't go away—*ever*. I would go so far as to say that, without help, a person who has been sexually abused can never have a healthy self-image or a life free of their past.

However, there is good news for those who struggle in this area. Thousands of people who have been sexually abused and sought assistance have been helped. If you are a victim of sexual abuse—or any other form of abuse—you are not alone. People all around you suffer with the same issues. They are probably dealing with their hurt in a similar way.

Here are four points anyone who has been sexually abused must hear:

1. It's not your fault.
2. Seek help. Don't suffer in silence.
3. There is hope.
4. God cares. He really does.

It's Not Your Fault

Sexual abuse is always the fault of the abuser. Sadly, most victims blame themselves for their trauma. It's time to put the blame in the proper place. If someone robbed you and stole your money, or if you were hit by a drunk driver, would you blame yourself? When you have been sexually abused in any way, you have become a victim of a horrible crime. The abuser is sick. If you blame yourself, then you will get sick too. *It's not your fault.*

Seek Help; Don't Suffer in Silence

The first step toward recovery is to seek help. Sometimes it's embarrassing. Other times you don't want to reveal a deep, dark family secret. The truth is, though, you will not get better if you don't seek help. If you choose to suffer in silence, you are choosing to get worse. You can't wish away your hurt. You are not the only one who has experienced this trauma. You *can* receive help from a qualified adult counselor.

Jill confided in her youth pastor that, six months prior, she had been at a party where an older guy forced her to have sexual intercourse with him. Jill said she felt "cheap and used," but she was afraid to tell anyone. She was even more afraid that, if she did tell someone, it would get back to the guy who abused her.

Her youth pastor did what the law required him to do and reported the rape. As the story unfolded, it was revealed that at least fifteen other girls had also been desecrated by this one young man. Jill received excellent support from a counselor who helped her. She dealt properly with the important issues that result from being violated. Jill's progress has been remarkably rapid. Had she waited longer to seek help, she may well have developed destructive behavioral patterns that would have taken years to undo. Victims need to seek help to prevent themselves from forever living in a state of turmoil. Please don't suffer alone.

I urge people who have been sexually abused not to wait another day, but to seek help immediately. If you have been sexually abused and have never sought help, then you are reading this chapter for a reason. I believe God wants you to seek help. Talk with someone.

There Is Hope!

If you have been hurt and hurt deeply, then it may be difficult for you to see that life will ever be different. You can draw hope from the knowledge that thousands before you have been set free from the pain after they sought help.

When Sandy was fourteen, her stepfather abused her in every way. Sandy told no one and acted as if nothing had happened. Her school work did not suffer; it even improved. No one knew her inner pain, until one day she took a bottle of her mother's prescription sleeping pills. When Sandy came to, she was in the hospital. She prayed she would die.

A good psychiatrist asked her if she would be willing to talk about why it hurt so bad that she wanted to die. He asked her if there was anyone she would talk to. Since I knew her, she asked for me. Sandy and I spent the next several hours together. She told me that she hated all guys. In her mind, her father had deserted her when she was eight years old. And now this stepfather, who had been a nice man, was sexually assaulting her. The pain went so deep that Sandy had lost all concept of hope.

Together we sought help. We reported this tragedy first to the psychiatrist and then to a social worker, who spoke to the mother and stepfather. Sandy went through extensive counseling, which helped her put her life together. Eventually she could see that she had been the victim of a very sick man. The counseling process gave her a reason to live—and a hope that life could be different.

Today, she isn't blaming herself. She still feels a tinge of pain when she thinks about the experience, but she has learned to move on. Not only does Sandy have two lovely children, but she and her husband also run a camp for battered and abused kids. She hung on to hope, and I'm sure she would tell you it was the right thing to do.

God Cares; He Really Does

Most people who have experienced any kind of sexual abuse struggle in their relationship with God. Under the circumstances, I can understand the difficulty they have comprehending the unconditional, sacrificial love of God in Jesus Christ. It's easy to blame God instead of allowing ourselves to be comforted by Him, but He wants to walk with us through hurts and disappointments.

The New Testament tells us how Jesus heard about the death of his friend Lazarus. When he saw the family grieving, *"Jesus wept"* (John 11:35). Jesus weeps for you too when you have been hurt.

Jesus knows a great deal about suffering. After all, He suffered a painful death on the cross, just to make it possible for you and me to spend an eternity with God in heaven. I believe that Jesus Christ would have suffered on the cross if you were the only person in the world who needed Him.

If God loves you enough to allow His only Son to die for you, then I believe He cares deeply for you and your pain. You need to understand that although it seems your circumstances may never change, your attitude *can* change—and that makes all the difference in the world.

If you have experienced sexual abuse, the battle is now in your hands. The choices are yours. You *can* overcome your pain. The decision to pursue wholeness is not always easy, but it is always the best.

The question I leave with you is this: Who and where do you want to be in ten years?

The decisions you make today will affect you the rest of your life. Choose health and wholeness; and remember, God walks with you through your darkest times.

What Is Sexual Abuse?

The following information about sexual abuse is something I distribute when I'm speaking to students about this important but horrible subject.[1]

Nobody has the right to touch your body in a sexual way without your permission, regardless of how much he or she loves you, how much money they have spent on you, or for any other reason.

Any time a touch makes you feel uncomfortable, you have the right to say no. You never *owe* another person the right to touch you. Trust your gut feelings. Pressuring, exploiting, or abusing another person is never acceptable in any relationship.

If someone touches you in a way you don't like, tell that person to stop and get away, and then talk about it with an adult you trust.

If an adult or older teenager has touched you in the past, it is *not your fault*. It is *always* the abuser's responsibility.

It is *very important* that you get counseling for sexual abuse *now*, to prevent problems as you grow older. If you have never talked with a counselor, seek help immediately.

The sexual assault of a person occurs when a male or female is tricked, coerced, seduced, intimidated, manipulated into cooperating, or forced into not offering resistance to sexual activity with another person.

Sexual abuse can be defined as:

- Showing children pornographic materials
- Taking nude pictures
- An adult exposing themselves to a child or asking the child to expose himself or herself
- Fondling private areas of the body
- Intimate kissing
- Genital contact
- Intercourse
- Rape

Sexual assault includes incest, molestation, rape, and "date rape."

Incest is sexual activity between any relatives. Usually this activity is started by a father or stepfather, grandfather, uncle, cousin, or brother. Occasionally it will be started by a mother, grandmother, or aunt.

Molestation is sexual activity with someone outside the person's family. Eighty percent of molestations are by someone the victim knows and trusts: a family friend, the mother's boyfriend, a neighbor, a teacher, a coach, a doctor or dentist, a pastor or priest, a youth leader, a camp counselor, or a baby-sitter. Only 20 percent of molestations are done by strangers.

Rape is forced penetration (by penis or any object) of the vagina, mouth, or anus against the will of the victim.

Acquaintance rape or *"date rape"* is rape by someone you know or are dating. Date rapists generally use just enough force to gain compliance. A man may use his physical power to have intercourse or take advantage of a situation by using force, pressure, deception, trickery, or teen vulnerability. The date rapist is not a weird, easily identifiable person. He is just like anyone else—except that he uses force to get his way. About 75 percent of teen rapes are acquaintance or date rapes.

What to Do If You Are Raped

If you are raped:

1. Get to a safe place.
2. *Do not* bathe, wash your private parts, or change clothes.
3. Call a rape crisis hotline.
4. Go to the hospital emergency room. Have a friend or family member go with you to the hospital and take a change of clothes if possible. Do this as soon as possible in order to:
   - Preserve the evidence.
   - Determine the extent and nature of physical injury and receive treatment.
   - Test for STDs and pregnancy.

Reasons for Reporting the Rape

Reporting the crime to police is a decision that only you can make. However, making a police report will greatly benefit you. Reporting the assault is a way of regaining your sense of personal power and control, as it enables you to do something concrete about the crime committed against you. Reporting the crime also helps ensure that you receive the best assistance available.

Making a police report will help prevent other people from being raped. Reporting and prosecuting the assailant are essential to prevent rape. Most rapists have raped more than one person. If the rape is not reported, the rapist cannot be caught.

I know this is a hard chapter to read. Actually, it is a very hopeful chapter if you think about it. If you have ever been sexually abused in any way, you can get help. Sure, it is difficult to talk with someone about it, but there is great benefit to your life and definitely your future. If you have never known the trauma of abuse, then reading this chapter can help you take the necessary precautions to help keep from being violated. At one time I hesitated to include this chapter in *The Purity Code*. After all, much of making a commitment to the Purity Code is a decision you make. Most times with sexual abuse, it is not about a decision you made. Just know that if any of this chapter describes your life in any way, there is help and there is hope. Do the courageous thing and seek help. You will not regret it.

Discussion Starters

1. A chapter on sexual abuse in a book on the Purity Code?! Why do you think this chapter needed to be written and discussed?

2. Why do you think sexual abuse is so much more prevalent in our society today than when your parents were kids?
3. What are practical ways a person can be less at risk towards sexual abuse?
4. What advice would you give to a friend who has experienced the devastation of sexual abuse?

General Questions About the Purity Code

1. Now that you have read the book, what decisions and commitments about the Purity Code have you made?
2. What decisions can you make on a regular basis to help you live by the Code?
3. How can God become more a part of your sexuality?
4. Have you made a commitment to live by the Purity Code? If so, when? Do you feel comfortable signing the Purity Code Pledge? (It is presented on the next page, but you can also print it out from *www.homeword.com*.)

HOME WORD

ENCOURAGING PARENTS, BUILDING FAMILIES

Do you not know that your body is a temple of the Holy Spirit, who is in you, whom you have received from God? You are not your own; you were bought at a price. Therefore honor God with your body.

(1 Corinthians 6:19–20)

The Purity Code Pledge

In honor of God, my family, and my future spouse, I commit my life to sexual purity. **This involves:**

- Honoring God with my **body**.
- Renewing my **mind** for the good.
- Turning my **eyes** from worthless things.
- Guarding my **heart** above all else.

Signature:_____ Date:_____

Notes

Chapter 2

1. *National Youth Risk Behavior Survey,* www.cdc.gov/mmwr/PDF/SS/
SS5505.pdf

2. *CDC, Sexual Behavior and Selected Health Measures: Men and Women 15–44
Years of Age, United States, 2002,* www.cdc.gov/nchs/data/ad/ad362.pdf

Chapter 3

1. This is obviously an oversimplification of the process. For a more in-depth
look, I recommend that your parents find a book, Web site, or pamphlet
that solely focuses on this process.

Chapter 4

1. S. J. Ventura, J. C. Abma, W. D. Mosher, and S. K. Henshaw, "Recent
Trends in Teenage Pregnancy in the United States, 1990-2002," In *Health
E-stats* (Hyattsville, MD: National Center for Health Statistics, 2006).

2. Hayley DiMarco, *Technical Virgin* (Grand Rapids, MI: Revell, 2006),
101.

3. Ibid., 100.

Chapter 5

1. Shannon Ethridge and Stephen Arterburn, *Every Young Woman's Battle* (Colorado Springs, CO: Waterbrook Press, 2004), 130–31.

Chapter 6

1. Jim Burns, *10 Building Blocks for a Happy Family* (Ventura, CA: Regal Books), 50.

Chapter 8

1. Help for pornography-related problems is available at *www.pureintimacy. org,* Focus on the Family (800–232–6459), or Christian Counsel (888–891–4673).

Chapter 9

1. Hayley DiMarco, *Sexy Girls, How Hot Is Too Hot?* (Grand Rapids, MI: Revell, 2006), 99.
2. 1 Corinthians 15:33. *Contemporary English Version* says: "Don't fool yourselves. Bad friends will destroy you."
3. Luke 11:34: "Your eye is the lamp of your body. When your eyes are good, your whole body also is full of light. But when they are bad, your body also is full of darkness."
4. DiMarco, *Sexy Girls*, 105.
5. Pam Stenzel, *Sex Has a Price Tag* (Grand Rapids, MI: Zondervan, 2003).

Chapter 11

1. DiMarco, *Technical Virgin*, 101.
2. Stenzel, *Sex Has a Price Tag*, 80.
3. Ibid., 88.

Chapter 13

1. Jim Burns, "General Information on Sexual Abuse," *www.homeword.com/ Articles.*

JIM BURNS, PhD, founded the ministry of HomeWord in 1985 with the goal of bringing help and hope to struggling families. As host of the radio broadcast *HomeWord With Jim Burns*, which is heard daily in over eight hundred communities, Jim has a passion to build God-honoring families through communicating practical truths that will enable adults and young people alike to live out their Christian faith.

In addition to the radio program, Jim speaks to thousands around the world each year through seminars and conferences. He is an award-winning author, whose books include *The Purity Code, Teaching Your Children Healthy Sexuality, Confident Parenting*, and *Creating an Intimate Marriage*.

Jim and his wife, Cathy, and their three daughters and son-in-law live in Southern California.

HOMEWORD

WHERE PARENTS GET REAL ANSWERS

Get Equipped with HomeWord...

Parent and Family Resources from HomeWord

Parenting Teenagers for Positive Results

This popular resource is designed for small groups and Sunday schools. The kit includes a DVD to begin each of the six sessions featuring a real family situation played out in humorous family vignettes followed by words of wisdom by youth and family expert, Jim Burns, Ph.D., from HomeWord. Each DVD session averages 5 minutes.

The kit contains:
DVD, CD with printable leader's guides and participant guides.

Creating an Intimate Marriage

Jim Burns wants every couple to experience a marriage filled with A.W.E.: affection, warmth, and encouragement. He shows husbands and wives how to make their marriage their priority as they discover ways to repair the past, communicate and resolve conflict, refresh their marriage spiritually, and more!

Confident Parenting

This is a must-have resource for today's family. Let Jim Burns help you to tackle overcrowded lives, negative family patterns, while creating a grace-filled home and raising kids who love God and themselves.

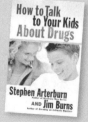

How to Talk to Your Kids About Drugs

Kids can't avoid being exposed to drug use today, some as early as grade school. Packed with practical information and time-proven prevention techniques, this book is a realistic, up-to-date, comprehensive plan for drug-proofing your kids. And if you suspect your kids are already using drugs and alcohol, respected counselor Steve Arterburn and well-known parenting and family expert Jim Burns offer step-by-step advice to get them straight and sober.

Tons of helpful resources for parents and youth.
Visit our online store at www.HomeWord.com
Or call us at 800-397-9725

Devotionals from Jim Burns
for you and your kids...

ONE LIFE
50 Powerful Devotions for Students

Jim Burns

One Life

Your kids only have one life – help them discover the greatest adventure life has to offer! 50 fresh devotional readings that cover many of the major issues of life and faith your kids are wrestling with such as sex, family relationships, trusting God, worry, fatigue and daily surrender. And it's perfect for you and your kids to do together!

Addicted to God

Is your kids' time absorbed by MySpace, text messaging and hanging out at the mall? This devotional will challenge them to adopt thankfulness, make the most of their days and never settle for mediocrity! Fifty days in the Scripture is bound to change your kids' lives forever.

Devotions on the Run

These devotionals are short, simple, and spiritual. They will encourage you to take action in your walk with God. Each study stays in your heart throughout the day, providing direction and clarity when it is most needed.

90 Days Through the New Testament

Downloadable devotional. Author Jim Burns put together a Bible study devotional program for himself to follow, one that would take him through the New Testament in three months. His simple plan was so powerful that he was called to share it with others. A top seller!